Hakik

BELIEF AND ISLAM

THE ANNOTATED TRANSLATION OF

ITIQAD-NAMA

by

The great *wali* (one loved by *Allahu Taala*), a treasure of *Allahu Taala*'s blessings, a superior person in every respect, master of unattainable knowledge, a light of the right, truth and the Religion

MAWLANA DIYA AD-DIN KHALID AL-BAGHDADI

(1778-1826)

Prepared by:

HÜSEYN HİLMİ IŞIK

Forty-Second Edition

Hakikat Kitabevi/Publishing
Darussefeka Cad. 53/A PK: 35
34083 Fatih, ISTANBUL/TURKEY
Tel: 90.212.523 4556 Fax: 90.212.523 3693
www.hakikatkitabevi.com
e-mail: info@hakikatkitabevi.com
JANUARY-2025

THE AUTHOR

Mawlana Diya ad-Din Khalid al-Baghdadi al-Uthmani (*quddisa sirruh*), the author of the book *Itiqad-nama,* was born in Shahrazur in the north of Baghdad in 1778/1192 AH and died in Damascus in 1826/1242. He was called 'al-Uthmani' because he was a descendant of Uthman Dhun Nurain, the Third Caliph (*radiy-Allahu Taala anh*, 'May *Allahu Taala* be pleased with him'). While teaching the celebrated ***Hadith al-Jibril,*** which is the second *hadith sharif* (a saying of the Prophet Muhammad *alayhis-salam*) in *Al-Arbaun an-Nawawiyya* by the great scholar an-Nawawi, to his younger brother *Hadrat* (expression of honor and respect used for Alahu Taala, the Prophet and scholars) Mawlana Mahmud Sahib, his brother requested him to write a commentary to that *hadith.* Mawlana Khalid, to please his brother's enlightened heart, accepted the request and explained the *hadith ash-sharif* in Persian in a book entitled *Itiqad-nama.* Its Turkish translation, *Herkese Lazım Olan Iman*, was translated into English (the present version *Belief and Islam*), French (*Foi et Islam*) and German (*Glaube und Islam*) in 1969 and later into several other languages, such as Tamil, Yoruba, Hausa, Malayalam and Danish. May *Allahu Taala* bless the innocent youth with reading this book and learning the correct *itiqad* (*iman, aqaid, furu*; Islamic beliefs, faith, creed, tenets) conveyed by the scholars of *Ahl as-Sunna*!

Printed at:

Ihlas Gazetecilik A.S.
Merkez Mah. 29 Ekim Cad. Ihlas Plaza No: 11 A/41
34197 Yenibosna-ISTANBUL, TURKEY
Tel: 90.212.454 3000

ISBN: 978-605-66709-8-5

PUBLISHER'S NOTE

Anyone who wishes to print this book in its original form or to translate it into any language is granted permission beforehand to do so; and those who undertake this beneficial endeavor are accredited with the prayers that we offer in advance to *Allahu Taala* in their name and also our best wishes of gratitude and we thank them very much. However, permission is subject to the conditions that the translation is accurate and true to the text, that the paper used in printing is of a good quality and that the design of the text is properly and neatly done without mistakes.

The prayer ***"Subhan-Allahi wa bi-hamdihi subhan-Allahil azim,"*** (called '*kalimat tanzih*') causes one's sins to be forgiven and protects one against resuming sinning when said a hundred times in the morning and in the evening. This prayer is quoted in the letters 307 and 308 of the book ***Al-Maktubat*** of the great *wali* and scholar *Al-Imam ar-Rabbani* (*quddisa sirruh*).

Ya Rahman, ya Rahim, ya Afuwwu ya Karim (saying these Names of *Allahu Taala*, one prays for His Graciousness, Mercy, Easy-forgiving, Generosity).

[A *salawat* (invocation) expressing praise and blessings upon Prophet Muhammad (*alayhis-salam*)]: "*Wa sall-Allahu ala Sayyidina Muhammadin wa ala Al-i Muhammad wa barik ala Sayyidina Muhammadin wa ala Al-i Muhammad. Allahumma Rabbana atina fid-dunya hasanatan wa fil-akhirati hasanatan wa qina adhaban-nar bi-rahmatika ya Arham ar-Rahimin! Amin!*"

Dear Reader, *As-salamu alaykum wa rahmatullah.*

Hakikat Publishing, located in Fatih, Istanbul, is committed to teaching our faith, Islam, thus causing an appreciation of Islam. May *Allahu Taala* be pleased with those who help us! *Amin* (Amen!)

Missionaries strive to promulgate Christianity; Jews spread the teachings in the ***Talmud***, and Freemasons try to annihilate all religions. Hakikat Publishing endeavors to disseminate Islam. A person with wisdom, knowledge and conscience understands the right one among these and, helping in its dissemination, causes happiness of the whole humanity in both worlds.

All the writings in this book have been translated from books written by Islamic scholars. Nothing has been added by the editor. We have undertaken this endeavor for the purpose of serving humankind and attaining the attention of those who protect people's rights. When you read the writings of these great and universally celebrated scholars with due attention and consideration, you will attain both material and immaterial knowledge which is useful, *insha-Allahu Taala* (if *Allahu Taala* wills). We extend our regards and love to you. May *Allahu Taala* bless you with good health and a pleasurable and beneficial life! *Amin*!

Hakikat Publishing

FOREWORD

Let us begin the book with the Basmala,
The Name 'Allah' is the best shelter.
His favors are immeasurable and countless,
He is the Creator loving to forgive, very compassionate.

Allahu Taala has Mercy upon all people on the earth; creating the things they need, He sends them to everybody. He shows the way that leads to endless bliss. He guides to the right path whomever He wishes among those who left the true way and followed the way to ***kufr*** (unbelief; disbelief in Islam) and heresy as a result of being deceived by their own ***nafs*** (a malignant force in humans that is hostile to *Allahu Taala*), evil company, books and other media that are harmful, saving them from eternal perdition. *Allahu Taala* does not bestow this blessing upon those who are cruel and exceed the limits, allowing them to stay on the way of *kufr*, which they like and desire. In the next world, *Allahu Taala* will forgive whoever is chosen of those guilty Believers who are to go to Hell and will admit them to Paradise. *Allahu Taala* alone creates every living creature, keeps every being in existence every moment and protects all against fear and horror. Trusting ourselves to the honorable Name of *Allahu Taala*, that is to say expecting help from Him, we begin to write this book.

May ***hamd*** (praise, gratitude) be to *Allahu Taala*! Peace and blessings be upon His beloved Prophet Muhammad (*alayhis-salam*). May beneficial prayers be on that Supreme Prophet's decent family (*Ahl al-Bayt*) and on each of his just and devoted Companions (*as-Sahabat al-Kiram*).

Hamd means believing and saying that *Allahu Taala* creates and sends all favors. ***Shukr*** means using all favors in conformity with Islam.

Thousands of valuable books have been written on the beliefs of the Islamic faith and its commands and prohibitions, and many of them have been translated into foreign languages and distributed to every country. On the other hand, ill-willed and short-sighted people, *zindiqs* (disbelievers pretending to be Muslims) and ignorant people of religious positon who have been deceived by

British spies have continuously attacked the useful, bountiful, lightsome rules of Islam and have striven to blemish and change it and to deceive Muslims.

However, it is being observed with gratitude that in almost every country scholars of Islam are still striving to spread and defend the Islamic faith. The scholars of the right path who, having heard from the *Sahabat al-Kiram*, wrote about Islam in books are the **scholars of *Ahl as-Sunna*.** Unsuitable speeches and articles, on the other hand, are being witnessed, which are claimed to have been taken from, but in reality which have been misinterpreted from, the *Quran al-Karim* and the *Hadith ash-Sharif* by few people who have not read or understood books written by the scholars of *Ahl as-Sunna*, yet these speeches and articles have proven to be ineffective against the firm *iman* of our Muslim brothers and sisters and have had no influence, except indicating the ignorance of their agents.

A person who declares to be a Muslim or who has been seen performing the ritual prayers (*salat*) in congregation (*jamaa*) must be looked on as a Muslim. If, later on, in their speech, writing or behavior something is seen disagreeing with the knowledge of *iman* as conveyed by the scholars of *Ahl as-Sunna*, they will be told that it is disbelief (*kufr*) or heresy (*bida*). They will be told to discontinue it and to repent.[1] If, with their short mind and coarse reasoning, they answer that they will not, it will be understood that they are heretics or ***murtadd*s** (renegades or apostates who have abandoned Islam) or people who have sold themselves out to British disbelievers. Even if they continue performing the ritual prayers, go on pilgramage and do all kinds of worship and good deeds, they will not escape from this disaster; unless they abandon things which cause disbelief and repent, they will not be Muslims. By learning well the things that cause disbelief, all Muslims should protect themselves from becoming renegades and should recognize well the disbelievers and those liars who pretend to be Muslims, especially the British spies, and keep away from their harm.

Rasulullah (*sall-Allahu alayhi wa sallam*) stated in a *hadith sharif* that wrong, false meanings would be extracted from the

---

[1] Repenting (***tawba***) means regretting, for having commited a sin or saying a statement or doing an action causing unbelief, and deciding not to do again. Begging *Allahu Taala* for forgiveness of one's sins is ***istighfar*** (saying '*Astaghfirullah*'). *Tawba* and *istighfar* should be done by heart, tongue and the organ that has committed the sin: the heart should regret; the tongue should pray and beg; the organ should ommit committing.

Quran al-Karim and the *Hadith ash-Sharif,* and thus 72 heretical groups would appear. This *hadith sharif* is explained in the books *Al-Bariqa* and *Al-Hadiqa*, which quote it on the authority of [the two celebrated books of the *Hadith*] *Al-Bukhari* and *Muslim.* We should not believe books and lectures of people among these heretical groups who come forward under such names as 'great scholar of Islam' or 'professor of religion', and we should be very alert not to fall into the traps of these thieves of faith and belief. Besides these unlearned Muslims, communists, freemasons and Christian missionaries, on the one hand, *Wahhabis* who have sold themselves to British plotters and Jewish Zionists, on the other, are striving to mislead Muslim children by various new methods. They are doing their best to annihilate *iman* and *islam* by way of fake articles, movies, theatres, radio and television broadcasts and web-sites. They are spending millions for this purpose. Islamic scholars (*rahimahum-Allah*) have, beforehand, given necessary responses to all of them and have shown *Allahu Taala*'s religion, the way to happiness and deliverance.

From among them, we have chosen the book *Itiqad-nama* by Mawlana Diya ad-Din Khalid al-Baghdadi al-Uthmani (*quddisa sirruh*), who was a distinguished scholar of Islam. ***Itiqad-nama*** was formerly translated into Turkish by the late honorable Haji Faizullah of Kemah, Erzincan, with the title ***Faraid al-fawaid*** and was printed in Egypt in 1894/1312. He lectured as a professor in the town of Soke, Türkiye, for many years and died in 1905/1323. This translation is simplified under the title ***Belief and Islam***. Its first edition was accomplished in 1966. To separate the text, our explanations are given in square brackets [ ]. We thank Allahu Taala infinitely for vouchsafing the lot of publishing this book. The original of ***Itiqad-nama*** is in Persian and is kept in the Istanbul University Library (Ibnul Emin Mahmud Kemal Section. F. 2639).

It is written at the end of the subject about 'disbeliever's marriage' in ***Ad-Durr al-mukhtar*** by virtuous Alauddin Haskefi (*rahimahu'llahu Taala*): "If a Muslim girl with *nikah* (religious marriage agreement) does not know Islam when she reaches puberty, the nikah becomes void [because she becomes an apostate by losing her *iman*]. The Attributes of Allahu Taala must be taught to her, and she must repeat them and say, 'I believe these.'" In explaining this, Ibn Abidin *(rahimahu'llahu Taala)* said:

> "When the girl is little, she belongs to her parents' faith; she is a Muslim. When she reaches puberty, she does not belong to her parents' faith any longer. When she reaches puberty while not knowing Islam, she becomes an apostate.

> Unless she learns and believes the six essentials of *iman* and *believes* that it is necessary to live up to [the essentials of] *islam*, she will not continue to be a Muslim even if she utters ***kalimat at-tawhid***, that is says, '***La ilaha illa'llah Muhammadun Rasulullah***' [meaning: '*Allahu Taala* exists and is One. Muhammad (*alayhis-salam*) is the Prophet sent by *Allahu Taala*.'] She has to learn and believe the six beliefs expressed [below] in '***Amantu bi'llahi...***' and she has to say, 'I accept the commands and prohibitions of *Allahu Taala*.'"

This explanation of Ibn Abidin shows that a disbeliever becomes a Muslim as soon as they say *kalimat at-tawhid* and believe briefly in its meaning, and, like any other Muslim, at the soonest possible time, one has to memorize the essentials of ***Amantu***[1] in the following statement and learn precisely their meaning and the necessary Islamic teachings: "***Amantu bi'llahi wa malaikatihi wa kutubihi wa rusulihi wal yawmil akhiri wa bil qadari khairihi wa sharrihi min-Allahi Taala wal bathu badal-mawti haqqun, ash-hadu an la ilaha illa'llah wa ash-hadu anna Muhammadan abduhu wa Rasuluhu.***" Also, if a Muslim child does not learn these six beliefs and Islamic teachings and does not say that he or she believes them, he or she becomes an apostate after reaching discretion and puberty. After [learning and believing them and thereby] attaining *iman*, it immediately becomes obligatory (*fard*) for one to inquire and learn **Islamic teachings**, that is the ordinances (***fard*s**) and prohibitions (***haram*s**), how to perform the ablutions (***wudu*** and ***ghusl***) and the ritual prayers (***salat***), and how to cover his or her intimate (*awrat*) body parts (see pp 27-29). When one asks a person about these teachings, it becomes *fard* for that person to teach them or to advise a true Islamic book. In case where there is no one to ask or no true book is found, it becomes *fard* for oneself to search. One becomes a disbeliever if searching is not done. Until finding, it is an excuse (*udhr*) not to know these teachings. A Muslim who does not perform acts of *fard* within their known times and/or commits *harams* will be subjected to torture in Hell. This work contains detailed information on the six essentials of *iman*. Every Muslim should read this book well and do their best to get their children and all their acquaintances to read it.

In the text, meanings of *ayat*s are given as ***maal*** (as reported by the scholars of ***tafsir***, science of explanation of the *Quran al-Karim*). Meanings of *ayat*s were understood only by *Rasulullah* (*sall-Allahu*

---

[1] These are the six essentials of belief explained in the chapter 'Essentials of *Iman*', p 30.

alayhi wa sallam) who, in the *hadith*s, taught these meanings to the *Sahaba*. The scholars of *tafsir* differentiated these *hadith*s from false ones fabricated by those people of religious position, who were *la-madhhabi* (those following none of the four *madhhab*s of *Ahl as-Sunna*; non-Sunnis), that is *munafiq*s and *zindiq*s who had sold themselves out to the British disbelievers. In the case that they could not find any *hadith*s, they themselves gave meanings to those *ayat*s by applying the science of *tafsir*. What is understood by those who speak Arabic but are unlearned in Islamic sciences and have no knowledge of *tafsir* is not called the *tafsir* of the *Quran*. In fact, a *hadith sharif* says: "**A person who gives meanings to the *Quran al-Karim* according to their own understanding becomes a disbeliever.**"

Presently, Muslims the world over have parted into three main groups. The first group consists of the true Muslims who have been following in the *Sahaba*'s footsteps. They are called ***Ahl as-Sunna*** or **Sunni Muslims** (Sunnis) or the ***Firqat an-najiyya,*** which means the group who will be protected from Hell. The second group is comprised of the enemies to the *Sahaba*, and they are called the ***Shii*s** (Shiites, Shia) or the ***Firqat ad-dalla*** (the heretical group). The third group is hostile both to the Sunnis and to the Shiis; they are called ***Wahhabi*s** or ***Najdi*s**, because they first appeared in the region of Najd in Arabia. They are also called the ***Firqat al-maluna*** (the accursed group), because, as written in our publications ***Endless Bliss*** and ***The Rising and the Hereafter***, they call Muslims 'disbelievers', and our Prophet cursed those who would call Muslims as such. Partition of Muslims into these three groups was caused by the Jews and the British.

Every Muslim should always say, "***La ilaha illa'llah***," for the *tazkiya* (purification) of their *nafs*, that is for cleansing themselves from sins and ignorance, which is inherent in their nature, and always repeat the prayer, "***Astaghfirullah***," for the *tasfiya* (refining) of their heart, that is for saving themselves from unbelief and sinfulness, which stem from their *nafs*, the Devil, bad friends and harmful books. Prayers said by one who obeys Islam and who repents are acceptable by *Allahu Taala*. If a person does not perform the *salat*, looks at unveiled women (without *hijab*) or at others' uncovered *awrat* parts or eats and drinks *haram* things, it is concluded that they do not obey Islam. Their prayers will not be accepted.

A glossary of Arabic and other non-English terms foreign to the English reader is appended. Number of years are given first in the Gregorian and then in Islamic, that is *Hijri* (of the Hegira) Lunar

(AH), calendars.

All the books published in various languages by Hakikat Publishing are being spread worldwide by way of internet and as book distribution.

May *Allahu Taala* keep us all on the right path shown by the scholars of *Ahl as-Sunna*! May He protect us from believing in the deceitful, insidious lies of those that are ignorant of Islam and of the *la-madhhabi* people and *munafiq*s exploiting the names such as 'great scholar of Islam'!

Gregorian	***Hijri* Solar**	***Hijri* Lunar**
2001	**1380**	**1422**

INTRODUCTION

[For a blessed and beautiful beginning, Mawlana Khalid al-Baghdadi (*quddisa sirruh*) commenced his book by quoting the 17th letter in the third volume of ***Al-Maktubat*** of *Al-Imam ar-Rabbani* Ahmad al-Faruqi as-Sirhindi (*rahmatullahi alayh*, d. 1624/1034), who had written in that letter:]

> "I begin my letter with the Basmala. Infinite glory and gratitude be to *Allahu Taala* who bestowed upon us all kinds of favors and honored us by making us Muslims and valued us by making us the *Umma* of Muhammad (*sall-Allahu Taala alayhi wa sallam*), which is the highest blessing.
>
> "We should meditate and realize that *Allahu Taala* alone sends every favor upon everybody. He alone creates everything. He alone is the One who keeps every being in existence every moment. Superior and good qualities of humans are all His blessings and favors. Our life, reason, knowledge, strength, senses of seeing, hearing and speech are all from Him. He always is the One who sends innumerable blessings and favors. He is the One who rescues human beings from trouble and distress, who accepts prayers and keeps away grief and disaster. Only He creates all nutrients and causes them to reach us. His blessing is so bountiful that He does not cut off the nourishment of those who commit sins. His covering sins is so great that He does not disgrace, degrade or dishonor those who disobey His commands or do not abstain from His prohibitions. Being so forgiving, so merciful, He does not hurry in punishing those who deserve punishment and torture (*adhab*). *Allahu Taala* abundantly gives His blessings and favors both upon those whom are liked and those who are enemies. Nothing is spared from anybody. The highest, the most valuable of benefactions is His showing us the right path to happiness and deliverance, encouraging us not to go astray but rather to go to Paradise. *Allahu Taala* commands us to adapt

ourselves to our beloved Prophet (*sall-Allahu Taala alayhi wa sallam*) in order that we may attain all the infinite blessings, endless and inexhaustible pleasures in Paradise, and to attain His grace and love. So, His blessings are as obvious as the sun. The favors which come from others, in fact, come from Him. *Allahu Taala*, again, is the One who makes others intermediaries and gives wish, power and strength to do favors. For this reason, He is always the One who sends all blessings that come through all places and through all people. To expect favors from anybody except *Allahu Taala* is like asking for something from the custodian or asking for alms from the poor. The ignorant as well as the educated, blockheads as well as the intelligent know that what we say here is right and to the point, because the things said are obvious facts and it is not necessary even to think them over.

"It is a human duty for everyone to thank –as much as one can– *Allahu Taala*, Who bestowed these favors. It is a debt, a duty which wisdom commands. But it is not easy to carry out this thanksgiving due to Him, because humans, having been originally created out of nothing, are weak, needy, faulty and defective. *Allahu Taala* always and eternally exists and is far from defectiveness. Every kind of superiority belongs to Him. Humans have by no means any similarity or proximity to Him. Can humans, who are so inferior, thank such a supreme being as *Allahu Taala* in a manner worthy of His Dignity? There are so many things that humans consider beautiful and valuable, but He knows that they are evil and dislikes them. Things which we consider to be reverence or gratitude may be common things not liked at all. For this reason, humans, with their own defective mind and short sight, cannot find out the things that express gratitude and veneration to *Allahu Taala*. Unless the ways of thanking and respecting are among those shown by Him, acts that are considered as praising may be slanderous.

"So, the debt of gratitude and human duties to be performed and believed by human beings towards *Allahu Taala* with the heart, tongue and body were defined by *Allahu Taala* and coveyed to humanity by His beloved

Prophet (*sall-Allahu Taala alayhi wa sallam*)! The human duties which He showed and ordered are called ***islam***. One thanks Him by following the way His Prophet taught. *Allahu Taala* does not accept or like any thanks, any worship incompatible with or outside this way, because there are many things which humans consider good or beautiful but which Islam disapproves of and regards to be ugly.

"Thus, in thanking *Allahu Taala*, people who have reasoning should adapt themselves to *Hadrat* Muhammad (*alayhis-salam*). His way is called **Islam**. A person following Muhammad (*alayhis-salam*) is called a **Muslim**. Thanking *Allahu Taala*, that is following Muhammad (*alayhis-salam*), is called ***ibada*** (worship). Islamic teachings are of two parts: religious and scientific.[1] Religious teachings are also of two parts:

"1) Teachings that must be believed by heart, called ***usul ad-Din*** or teachings of ***iman***. In short, ***iman*** means believing the six essentials taught by Muhammad (*alayhis-salam*), to accept Islam and to avoid saying and using signs of disbelief (*kufr*). Every Muslim must learn the signs of disbelief and avoid using them. A person with *iman* is called a **Muslim**.

"2) Teachings of ritual practices that must be performed and of those that must not be avoided by the body and by the heart. Teachings that have to be performed are called ***fard***, and those things which are ordered to be avoided are called ***haram***. These teachings are called ***furu ad-Din*** or ***al-ahkam al-Islamiyya*** or **Islamic teachings."**

[Saying *kalimat at-tawhid* with believing its meaning is the first thing necessary for every person to do. *Kalimat at-tawhid* is, "***La ilaha illa'llah Muhammadun Rasulullah***," and it means: "*Allahu Taala* exists and is One. Muhammad (*alayhis-salam*) is the Prophet sent by *Allahu Taala*." Believing this fact means "having *iman*," and "becoming a Muslim." A person who has *iman* is called a '***Mumin***

[1] "Reformers" of Islam say that religious teaching are called 'scholastic teachings' and scientific teachings are called 'rational teachings'.

(Believer)' and a '**Muslim**'. *Iman* has to be continuous. Therefore, it is necessary to avoid doing acts that cause disbelief and using things that symbolize disbelief.

The ***Quran al-Karim*** is the *Kalam al-Ilahi* (Divine Speech, Word of *Allahu Taala*). *Allahu Taala* sent the *Quran al-Karim* to Muhammad (*alayhis-salam*) through the Archangel *Jabrail* (Gabriel, *alayhis-salam*). The words in the *Quran al-Karim* are in the Arabic language, and they were sent in *ayat*s (sentences, statements or verses), letters and words arranged together by *Allahu Taala*. The meanings carried by these letters and words convey the *Kalam al-Ilahi*. These letters and words are called the ***Quran al-Karim***. The meanings that disclose the *Kalam al-Ilahi* are the *Quran al-Karim* as well. This *Quran al-Karim* which is the *Kalam al-Ilahi* is not a creature. It is eternal in the past and everlasting, like the other Attributes of *Allahu Taala*. Once every year *Jabrail* (*alayhis-salam*) would visit to recite, in the same order as they had been recorded in the ***Lawh al-mahfuz*** (place where Divine Knowledge was recorded in eternal past), the part of the *Quran al-Karim* that had already been revealed, and our Prophet would repeat it. In the year when the Prophet was about to honor the hereafter, *Jabrail* (*alayhis-salam*) visited twice, reciting the entire *Quran al-Karim*. Our Prophet and most of the *Sahaba* had memorized the *Quran al-Karim* wholly. Before the end of the year when he honored the hereafter with his blessed being, Abu Bakr as-Siddiq, the Caliph, brought together those who had memorized the *Quran al-Karim* and having gathered those parts that had already been written, had a committee write down the entire *Quran al-Karim*. Thus a written copy called the ***mus'haf*** came about. Thirty-three thousand *Sahabi*s reached a consensus that every letter of that copy was in its right place.

The sayings of Muhammad (*alayhis-salam*) are called the ***Hadith ash-Sharif*** (pl. ***ahadith sharif***). A *hadith sharif* with meaning by *Allahu Taala* but with words by Muhammad (*alayhis-salam*) is termed a ***hadith qudsi***. There are many books of the *Hadith*. Those by ***Al-Bukhari*** and **Muslim** are the most widely known.

Of the commands of *Allahu Taala*, teachings that are to be believed are called ***iman***; those which must be performed are termed ***fard***, and prohibitions are termed ***haram***. *Fard*s and *haram*s are called the ***ahkam al-Islamiyya*** (the rules of Islam). A person who does not believe in even one of the Islamic teachings is called a ***kafir*** (disbeliever in Islamic beliefs).

The second necessary thing for a person to do is to purify their heart. The word 'heart' has two meanings. The piece of flesh in our chest is called 'heart' by almost all people. Heart in this sense exists in animals as well. The second 'heart' is the invisible, spiritual heart staying in the material heart. This second heart is also called 'heart'. It is this heart that is written in religious books. This heart is the place of Islamic teachings. It is this heart, again, which believes or disbelieves. A heart that believes is pure. A heart that disbelieves is dirty and is 'dead'. It is our first duty to purify the heart by striving hard. Worship, especially performing the ritual prayers (*salat*), and begging for forgiveness (*istighfar*), purifies the heart. Committing *haram*s dirties the heart. Our blessed Prophet stated: "**Say '*Astaghfirullah*' frequently! If one continues saying it, *Allahu Taala* protects one against all illnesses and disasters. He sends nourishment from places that one does not expect at all.**" *Istighfar* means saying, "***Astaghfirullah***" (May *Allahu Taala* forgive me!) In order for the prayer to be accepted, the supplicant must be a Muslim, repent for one's sins and say the prayer knowing its meaning and believing it. Prayers said with a darkened heart will not be accepted. Also, if one says one's prayer three times and continues performing the five daily *salat*, one's heart will become pure and begin saying the prayer by itself. A prayer said only with the mouth but without the heart will be of no use.

The religious teachings declared by the Islamic religion are the teachings written in the books of the scholars of *Ahl as-Sunna*. One becomes a disbeliever if one does not believe, among the teachings of *iman* (beliefs) and *islam* (rituals) conveyed by the scholars of *Ahl as-Sunna*, in any of the ***nass*** (general term for an *ayat karima* or a *hadith sharif*) with open meanings. One will be called a hypocrite (***munafiq***) if one hides one's disbelief. One is called a ***zindiq*** if one both hides one's disbelief and pretends to be a Muslim and thereby tries to deceive Muslims. Misbelieving that results from misinterpretation of the *nass* with unclear meaning does not cause one to become a disbeliever, but, because of deviating from the true way of *Ahl as-Sunna*, one will go to Hell. Owing to such person's belief in the *nasses* with open meanings, that person will not stay eternally in torture, being rescued from Hell and taken into Paradise. People of this sort are called heretics (***ahl al-bida***) or groups of heresy (***dalala***). Seventy-two heretical groups have appeared. None of the acts of worship or the favors or services to humanity performed by these people or by disbelievers or renegades will be acceptable or will do them any good in the hereafter. Muslims with correct belief are called ***Ahl as-Sunnat wal-Jamaa*** or **Sunni.** Sunni Muslims have differed in four *madhhabs* (see pp 71-72) in respect to performing their acts of worship. Followers of any one of the four *madhhabs* also know that the followers of the other three *madhhabs* also belong to *Ahl as-Sunna*, and they love one another. A person who is not in any of these four *madhhabs* is not a Sunni Muslim. A person who is not *Ahl as-Sunna* is either a disbeliever or a heretic.[1]

If a person who performs acts of worship according to one of the four *madhhabs* repents upon committing sins or upon making any mistakes in those acts of worship, that person will be forgiven. If one does not repent, *Allahu Taala* might, if He wills, forgive and might never put that person into Hell. If *Allahu Taala* wills He will torture that person as much as the committed sins of that person deserve but later that

---

[1] This is written in ***The Letters (Al-Maktubat)*** of *Al-Imam ar-Rabbani*, particularly in the 286th letter of the first volume, as well as in at-Tahtawi's annotation to the book ***Ad-Durr al-mukhtar*** (chapter entitled Zabayikh) and in ***al-Basair li-munkiri t-tawassuli bi ahli l-maqabir*** with documents. Last two books are in Arabic. The last one, having been originally written and printed in India, has been reproduced by Hakikat Publishing in Istanbul by offset process a number of times since 1975/1395.

person will be released from torture. One who does not believe even one of the clear teachings which are known to be essentially believed in Islam, that is which are known even by uneducated people, will be subjected to eternal torture in Hell. That person is called an disbeliever (***kafir***) or an apostate (***murtadd***).

There are two types of disbelievers: the *disbeliever* with a revealed, heavenly book, and the one without a book. If a person with Muslim parents later abandons Islam and becomes an unbeliever, that person is called an apostate (***murtadd***). Ibn Abidin (*rahimah-Allahu Taala*) wrote in the subject about 'those whose marriage is invalid because of polytheism': "*Murtadd*s, *mulhid*s, *zindiq*s, fire-worshippers (*Majusi*s), idolaters, ancient Greek philosophers, *munafiq*s, those followers of the 72 heretical groups in Islam whose heresy progressed into disbelief, Brahmins, Buddhists, Batinis, Ibahatis and Durzis (Druses) are all disbelievers without heavenly books." Communists and freemasons also are disbelievers without heavenly books. Those Jews and Christians who believe in the ***Tawrat*** (the original of the **Torah**/Old Testament) and the ***Injil*** (the original of the ***Bible***/New Testament), the revealed heavenly books which were later changed and spoiled, are disbelievers with books. If these disbelievers believe that there is an Attribute of Divinity in a creature, they become polytheists (***mushrik***s, people of *shirk*). The ***Sifat adh-Dhatiyya*** and the ***Sifat ath-Thubutiyya*** of *Allahu Taala* are called the Attributes of Divinity (***Uluhiyya***).

A disbeliever, with or without a heavenly book, who embraces Islam becomes a decent Muslim with no sin and escapes going to Hell, but that person has to become a Sunni Muslim. Becoming a **Sunni** Muslim means reading and learning a book written by one of the scholars of *Ahl as-Sunna* and adapting one's *iman*, acts and words to what one learns from that book. In the world it is understood from one's clear words said without *darura* (strong necessity or compulsion) and actions if one is a Muslim or not. It becomes definite at one's last breath if one goes to the next world with *iman*. If a male or female Muslim with serious sins repents with pure heart, their sins will surely be forgiven, becoming sinless and pure. It is explained in detail in books of *ilm al-hal* (for example, on p 6 of this text and in ***Endless Bliss***) what repentance (***tawba***) is and how to repent.]

IMAN AND ISLAM

In this book, ***Itiqad-nama***, a *hadith sharif* will be explained in which the Prophet (*sall-Allahu alayhi wa sallam*) told about ***iman*** and ***islam.*** I hope that, through the blessing of this *hadith sharif*, the belief of Muslims will be completed [strengthened], and thereby they will attain deliverance and happiness. Again I hope that it will cause me, Khalid [*quddisa sirruh*], whose sins are so many, to be saved.

May *Allahu Taala*, in Whom I have the beautiful belief that He needs nothing and that His favors and blessings are so plentiful and Who pities human creatures much, forgive this poor Khalid, whose stock is so little and heart so black, for my unsuitable words and accept my defective acts of worship. May *Allahu Taala* protect us against the evils of the deceitful, lying Satan [and against being deceived by false, erroneous words and writings of the enemies of Islam] and make us happy! He is the Most Merciful of the merciful and the Most Generous of the generous.

As stated by Islamic scholars, every male or female Muslim who have become responsible (***mukallaf;*** one who has reached discretion/*aqil* and adolescence/*baligh*) has [to acknowledge and know *Allahu Taala*, in other words,] to know and believe in ***as-Sifat adh-Dhatiyya***[1] (Personal Attributes) and ***as-Sifat ath-Thubutiyya*** of *Allahu Taala* correctly. It is this which is primarily obligatory (*fard*) for everybody. Not to know is not an excuse; it is a sin. I, Khalid ibn Ahmad al-Baghdadi, write this book not to make a show

---

[1] The six Attributes that are specific to *adh-Dhat* (Self, Essence, Person or Personality) of *Allahu Taala* are called ***as-Sifat adh-Dhatiyya.*** They are ***al-wujud***, *Allahu Taala*'s existence by Himself; ***al-Qidam***, being without a beginning and eternal in the past; ***al-Baqa***, existing without end and never to become nonexistent; ***al-Wahdaniyya***, having no partner, equal or match in any respect; ***al-Mukhalafatun lil-hawadith***, being dissimilar to every creature in every respect; and ***al-Qiyamu bi nafsihi***, *Allahu Taala*'s self-existence, being needy of nothing for eternal existence. No creature has any of these six attributes, nor any relation with them. Some Islamic scholars said that *al-Mukhalafatun lil-hawadith* and *al-Wahdaniyya* were the same and that the number of *as-Sifat adh-Dhatiyya* was five.

of superiority and knowledge to others or to become famous but to leave a reminder, a service, behind. May *Allahu Taala* help humble Khalid and all Muslims with His Power and through His Prophet's blessed soul! *Amin*!

Everything other than *Allahu Taala* is called the ***ma-siwa*** or ***alam*** (the universe). People call it '**nature**' now. All the worlds of beings were nonexistent. Allahu Taala is the One who has created them all. They all are ***mumkin*** and ***hâdith***.[1] The hadîth *ash-Sharif*, "***Allahu Taala* was existent; nothing else was existent**," expresses this fact.

A second evidence showing that creatures are *hâdith* is the fact that they are transforming and changing all the time. Everything is changing; however, something *qadim* (without a beginning, eternal in the past) should never change. *Adh-Dhat* of *Allahu Taala* and His Attributes are *qadim* and they never change.[2] The changes in creatures, their transforming to one another, cannot be coming from the eternity in the past. They should have a beginning and come into existence from elements or substances which must have been created out of nonexistence.

Another evidence for the fact that the universe is *mumkin*, that is it came into being out of nonexistence, is that creatures, as we see, are *hâdith*; that is they have been coming into existence out of nothing.

There are two beings: the ***mumkin*** and the ***Wajib* [*al-wujud*]**.[3] If only the *mumkin* existed, or if *Wajib al-wujud* did not exist, nothing

---

[1] The sign ^ over a vowel makes its pronunciation long. The word *hâdith* with this sign over the first vowel has a different meaning from that of 'hadîth' with the sign over the second vowel which means the 'saying' of the Prophet Muhammad (*alayhis-salam*). Due to its frequent use, 'hadîth' is written as '*hadith*' in this text. Here ***mumkin*** means 'that which may come into existence out of nonexistence and may become nonexistent while being existent', and ***hâdith*** means 'that which *came* into existence while being nonexistent; that created later'.

[2] However, in the universe the state of substances changes in physical events. In chemical reactions, the essence or structure of substances changes. We see objects or substances cease to exist and change into other substances. Today, in atomic changes and nuclear reactions, which have been discovered recently, the matter or element also ceases to exist and turns into energy.

[3] 'Wujud' means 'existence, being.' There are three kinds of existence. The first one is ***Wajib al-wujud***, the Necessary Existence. He always

would exist.[1] For this reason, the *mumkin* could not come into existence or go on being on its own. If some power had not affected it, it would have always remained in nonexistence and could not have come into existence. Since a *mumkin* could not create itself; it could not, naturally, create other *mumkin*s, either. That which has created the *mumkin* has to be *Wajib al-wujud*. The existence of the universe shows that a creator who created it out of nothing exists. So, the Unique Creator of all that are *mumkin*, the creatures, is the only *Wajib al-wujud* without being *hâdith* or *mumkin*, but always existent and eternal. '*Wajib al-wujud*' means that its existence is not from something else but from itself, that is it is always self-existent and is not created by someone else. Were this not the case, then it would have to be a creature (*mumkin* and *hâdith*) created by someone else. This is contrary to what is deduced above. In Persian '***Khuda***' [used as a name for *Allahu Taala*] means 'always self-existent, eternal in the past.'[2]

We see that the classes of beings are in an astounding order, and science discovers new laws of this order every year. The Creator of this order must be **Hayy** (Ever-living), **Alim** (All-knowing), **Qadir** (Almighty), **Murid** (All-willing), **Sami** (All-hearing), **Basir** (All-seeing), **Mutakallim** (All-speaking) and **Khaliq** (Creator),[3] because death, ignorance, incapability, compulsion, deafness, blindness and dumbness are all defects and imperfections. It is impossible that such defective attributes be existent in *Allahu Taala* Who has

---

exists. He has never been nonexistent before, nor will He stop existing in the everlasting future. Only *Allahu Taala* is *Wajib al-wujud*. The second one is ***mumtani al-wujud***, which cannot exist. It should always be nonexistent. Such is a partner to *Allahu Taala*; that is another god partner to *Allahu Taala* or resembling *Allahu Taala* can never exist. The third one is ***mumkin al-wujud***, that may or may not exist. So are the universe, all creatures without any exception. The opposite of wujud is ***'adam*** (non-existence). All creatures were in *'adam*, were nonexistent, before they came into existence.

[1] For it is a change, an event, to come into existence out of nonexistence, and, according to our knowledge in physics, in order for a change to take place in an object, the object has to be acted upon by an exterior power, the source of which has to precede the object.

[2] For detailed information please refer to the chapter "Allah Exists and is One" p. 92.

[3] These are the eight attributes of ***as-Sifat ath-Thubutiyya*** of *Allahu Taala*, that, besides existing in *Allahu Taala*, are partially present also in creatures.

created this universe (*alam*) or Creation (*kainat*) in such an order and Who protects them against annihilation.[1]

Moreover, we also see the above eight attributes of perfection [called ***as-Sifat as-Subutiyya*** existing partially] in creatures. *Allahu Taala* created them in creatures. If these attributes did not exist in Him, how could He create them in creatures? If these attributes did not exist in Him, those creatures would be superior to Him.

We should also add that the Creator of all worlds of beings ought to possess all the attributes of perfection and superiority and none of the attributes of deficiency, since one who is defective cannot be the Creator (*Khuda*).

Aside from these reasonable evidences, *ayat*s and *hadith*s explain clearly that *Allahu Taala* has perfect attributes. Therefore, it is not permissible to doubt it. Doubt causes disbelief. The above-mentioned eight perfect attributes are called the ***Sifat ath-Thubutiyya***. *Allahu Taala* has all the eight perfect attributes. There is no defect, disorder or change in His Person, Attributes or Deeds. The ***Sifat adh-Dhatiyya*** and *the* ***Sifat ath-Thubutiyya*** are called the Attributes of Divinity ***(Uluhiyya)***. If one believes that a creature possesses an attribute of divinity, one becomes a polytheist (***mushrik***).

---

[1] Every being, from atom to stars, has been created with some calculations and laws. The regularity in the known laws of physics, chemistry, astronomy and biology bewilders the human mind. Even Darwin had to say that when he had thought of the order and delicacy in the structure of the eye, he had felt as if he would go crazy. Air is a mixture of nitrogen (78%), oxygen (21%), and noble (inert) gases (1%). It is a mixture, not a compound. If oxygen content were more than 21 percent, it would burn our lungs. Were it less than that amount, it would be unable to burn the nutrients in blood. It would be impossible for human beings and animals to live. This percentage, 21, does not change anywhere, not even during rains. And this, in its turn, is a great blessing. Does it not show the Existence, Power and Grace of *Allahu Taala*? Construction of the eye is a mere nothing when compared with this wonder. Is it ever possible that the One who has created all the laws, delicate calculations and formulas taught as scientific knowledge would have defective attributes?

THE ESSENTIALS OF *ISLAM*

With the grace of *Allahu Taala*, Who keeps all creatures in existence every moment, Who is always omnipresent and overseeing and gives all the favors and gifts, now we begin to explain the blessed saying of our Prophet (*sall-Allahu alayhi wa sallam*).

Our beloved superior *Hadrat* Umar ibn al-Khattab (*radiy-Allahu Taala anh*), who was a heroic leader of Muslims, one of the highest Companions of the Prophet and was famous for his truthfulness, stated:

> "It was such a day that a few of us, the Companions, were in the presence and service of *Rasulullah* (*sall-Allahu alayhi wa sallam*)." That day, that hour, was so blessed, so valuable a day that one could hardly have the chance to live it once again. On that day, it fell to his lot to be honored with being in the Prophet's company and near him and to see his blessed face that was food, pleasure and comfort for souls. To emphasize the value and honor of that day, he said, "It was such a day..." Could there be another time as honorable and valuable as the one at which it falls to one's lot to see *Jabrail* (*alayhis-salam*) in the guise of a human being, to hear his voice and to hear the knowledge humans need as beautifully and clearly as possible through the blessed mouth of *Rasulullah* (*sall-Allahu Taala alayhi wa sallam*)?
>
> "At that hour, a man came near us like the rising of a full moon. His clothes were extremely white and his hair was very black. Signs of travel, such as dust and perspiration were not seen on him. None of us among the *Sahaba* of the Prophet (*sall-Allahu alayhi wa sallam*) recognized him, that is he was not one of the people we had seen or known before. He sat down in the Presence of *Rasulullah* (*sall-Allahu alayhi wa sallam*). He placed his knees near the Prophet's blessed knees." This person, in the guise of a human figure, was the angel named *Jabrail.* Although his way of sitting seemed incompatible with manners (*adab*), it showed us a very important fact: in learning religious knowledge, shyness had no place, nor did pride or arrogance become a master. With this behavior, *Hadrat Jabrail* wanted to show the *Sahaba* that everybody should ask what they wanted to know about Islam freely from teachers without feeling shy, for there should not be shyness in learning Islam or embarrassment in performing, teaching or learning one's duties towards *Allahu Taala.*

"That noble person put his hands on *Rasulullah*'s (*sall-Allahu alayhi wa sallam*) blessed knees. He asked *Rasulullah*: '**Oh Messenger of Allah! Tell me what Islam is and how to be a Muslim.**'"

Literal meaning of '***islam***' is 'to surrender in submission.' *Rasulullah* (*sall-Allahu Taala alayhi wa sallam*) explained that the word '***islam***' was the name of [the group of] five basic essentials in the religion of Islam, which are:

1. *Rasulullah* (*sall-Allahu alayhi wa sallam*) said that the first of the essentials of *islam* was "**saying *kalimat ash-shahada***" (the statement of testimony); that is to say one should say, "**Ashhadu an la ilaha illa'llah wa ashhadu anna Muhammadan abduhu wa *rasul*uh.**" In other words, a mentally mature person who has reached the age of puberty and who can talk has to say, **"On the earth and in the heavens, there is nothing nor anyone but *Allahu Taala* Who has the right to be worshipped and Who is worthy of deifying. The real Deity is *Allahu Taala* alone. He is the *Wajib ul-wujud.* Every kind of superiority exists in Him. No defect exists in Him. His name is Allah,"** and to believe in this absolutely with all their heart. And also one should say and believe: "**The most noble person named Muhammad *ibn*** [the son of] **Abdullah** who had a rosy, white-reddish, bright and lovely face with black eyes and brows, a blessed wide forehead and beautiful manners, whose shadow never fell on the ground and who was soft-spoken and was called Arab because he had been born in Mecca of Hashemite-descent, **is the human being and Messenger sent by *Allahu Taala*.**" The Prophet's mother was *Hadrat* Amina *bint* (daughter of) Wahab. His birth in Mecca honored the world [at the dawn of Monday, April 20, in the year 571]. When he was forty, he was informed that he was the Prophet [Monday, Ramadan 17, 610]. That was named the year of the '***Bitha***' (a prophet's being sent for calling people to the right path). After this, he invited people to Islam in Mecca for thirteen years. Then he migrated (the *Hijra*, Hegira) to Medina on the command of *Allahu Taala*. From there, he spread Islam everywhere. Ten years after the *Hijra*, he died in Medina on July 8, 632 (Monday, *Rabi al-Awwal* 12).[1]

---

[1] According to historians, the Prophet entered the cave at the Sawr Mountain towards evening on Thursday 27th of the month *Safar* in the Gregorian year 622, during his migration (the *Hijra*) from *al-Makkat al-Mukarrama* (the Honorable City of Mecca, the birthplace of Muhammad *alayhis-salam*) to *al-Madinat al-Munawwara* (the Illuminated City of Medina). He left the cave on Monday night and

2. The second of five essentials of *islam* is **"the performance of the *salat*** (ritual prayers) **when its time comes"** five times daily and fulfilling its *fards*." It is *fard* for every Muslim to perform the ***salat*** five times every day within the defined time of each prayer and to know that it is performed within its defined time. By following calendars that are wrongly prepared by ignorant or *la-madhhabi* (not following any of the four *madhhabs*; non-Sunni) people, performing a *salat* before its defined time is a great sin, and the *salat* performed as such is not valid. This also causes the initial *sunna* division of the noon prayer and the *fard* division of the sunset prayer to be performed within the time of *karaha* (periods of time in which performing *salat* is sinful). Time for a *salat* is understood by the muezzin's (*muadhdhin*, person calling Muslims to the *salat*) calling the *adhan* (call to the *salat*).[1] The *salat* has to be performed paying attention to its *fards*, *wajibs* and *sunnas* [various rules within any *salat*] before its defined time is over and submitting the heart to *Allahu Taala*. In the *Quran al-Karim*, ritual prayers are called the '***salat***', which means humans' praying, angels' saying *istighfar* and *Allahu Taala*'s showing compassion. In Islam, the ***salat*** means to do certain actions and to read certain things from memory as written in books of *ilm al-hal*. The *salat* is started with the ***takbir al-iftitah*** by saying the words '***Allahu akbar***' as the hands, for men, after being raised up to the ears are clasped under the navel and as they, for women, after being raised up to the level of the shoulders are placed over the breasts. It is completed by greeting [***salam,*** saying "*as-salamu alaykum wa rahmatu'llah*"] once while turning the head to

---

entered Quba, a quarter near Medina, on Monday 8th of the month *Rabi ul-awwal* (20th of September in Gregorian calendar and 7th of September in Julian calendar). This happy day became the beginning of Muslims' *Hijri* (of the *Hijra*) Solar (*Shamsi*) calendar. The beginning of the *Hijri Solar* calendar adopted by the Shiites had been six months earlier than this; that is it starts with the *Nawruz* festival of the fire-worshipping disbelievers (*Majusis*, Zoroastrians, Parsees, Mazdean) on March 20. The Prophet stayed at Quba until Thursday, when duration of the day was equal to that of the night all over the world, and left the quarter on Friday, entering Medina the same day. The outset of the month of *Muharram* in the same year (Friday, 16th of July) was accepted as the beginning of *Hijri* Lunar (*Qamari*) calendar. The *Hijri Solar* year in which a Gregorian year starts is 622 years shorter than that new year, and the Gregorian year in which a *Hijri Solar* year starts is 621 years longer than that new year.

[1] Vocalization of it by disbelievers or heretics or through loudspeakers is not called the *adhan al-Muhammadi* (the 'call of Muhammad' to the *salat*).

the right and once to the left shoulders at the end of the last sitting position.

3. The third of the five essentials of *islam* is "**giving the *zakat* of one's property**." The literal meaning of *zakat* is 'purity, praising, and becoming good and beautiful.' In Islam, ***zakat*** means 'for one who has property of *zakat* more than one's needs and at an amount of or exceeding the certain limit called the ***nisab*** to separate a certain amount of one's property and give it to those Muslims defined in the *Quran al-Karim* without embarrassing them.' *Zakat* is given to seven kinds of people. There are four types of *zakat* in all the four *madhhabs*: the *zakat* of gold [including equivalent of banknotes] and silver, the *zakat* of commercial goods, the *zakat* of four-legged animals of butchery that graze in the fields for more than half a year, and the *zakat* of crops obtained from the soil. This fourth type of *zakat*, called ***ushr***, is paid as soon as the crop is harvested. The other three are paid one year after they reach the amount of nisab.

4. **"Fasting (*sawm*) during every day of the month of Ramadan"** is the fourth essential of *islam*. Fasting is called '***sawm***,' which means protecting against three things [during the days] of the month of Ramadan, as they were commanded by *Allahu Taala*: eating, drinking and intercourse. The month of Ramadan begins upon seeing the new moon on the [western] horizon. It may not begin at the time calculated in calendars beforehand.

5. The fifth essential of *islam* is "**the performing of the pilgrimage (*hajj*) by able persons once in their life**." For people who have money enough for going to and coming back from the city of Mecca including an amount sufficient for the subsistence of the family they leave behind until they come back, it is *fard* once in their lifetime to perform *tawaf* around the Kaaba and to perform *waqfa* on the plain of Arafat, provided that the way is safe and they are physically healthy.

"Upon hearing these answers from *Rasulullah*, that person said, '**Oh! *Rasul-Allah*! You have told the truth**.' " *Hadrat* Umar (*radiy-Allahu anh*) said that the *Sahabis* who were present were astonished at the behavior of this person who asked a question and confirmed that the answer was correct. One asks with a view to learning what one does not know; but to say, "You have told the truth," indicates that one already knows it.

The highest of the five essentials listed above is saying and believing the meaning of **kalimat ash-shahada.** The next highest is performing the *salat*. Next to this is fasting. Then comes the *hajj*.

The last one is giving the *zakat*. It is unanimously certain that *kalimat ash-shahada* is the highest. About the sequence of the other four, most scholars of Islam said the same as the foregoing. *Kalimat ash-shahada* was the first to become *fard* at the beginning of Islam. *Salat* five times daily became *fard* during the *Miraj* (the event of the Prophet Muhammad's Ascension) in the twelfth year of *Bitha*, a year and some months before the Hegira. Fasting during Ramadan became *fard* in the month of Shaban, the second year of the Hegira. Giving zakat became *fard* in the month of Ramadan, in the same year when fasting became *fard*. And *hajj* became *fard* in the ninth year of the Hegira.

If one disbelieves, refuses to accept, makes fun of or shows disrespect for one of these five essentials of *islam*, one becomes a disbeliever (may *Allahu Taala* protect us!) Similarly, one who does not accept any of the things which are unanimously and clearly declared to be *halal* (permitted) or *haram* (forbidden), or who says '*halal*' about *haram* or '*haram*' about *halal*, becomes a disbeliever. If one disbelieves or dislikes one of the inevitably known Islamic teachings, that is teachings that are heard and known even by uneducated people that live in Muslim countries, one becomes a disbeliever.

[For example, eating pork, having alcoholic drinks, *gambling* and, for a woman or girl, showing herself to others with nothing to cover her head, hair, arms and legs and, for a man, showing himself to others without covering the part between the knees and the navel are all *haram*. In other words, *Allahu Taala* has forbidden these acts. The four authentic *madhhab*s, which explain the commands and prohibitions of *Allahu Taala*, described differently the intimate, private body parts (***awrat***) of the male body that are *haram* to look at or to show to others. It is *fard* for every Muslim to cover those parts of the body described by the *madhhab* they belong to. It is *haram* for others to look at those who have not covered these parts of their bodies. It is written in ***Kimya as-Saada*** that it is *haram* for women and girls to go out without covering their heads, hair, arms and legs, and it is also *haram* to go out with thin, ornamented, tight and perfumed dresses. Their mothers, fathers, husbands and brothers who give permission, consent or approval to their going out as such will share the sin and penalty (*adhab*); that is they will burn in Hell together. If they repent, they will be forgiven and will not be burned. *Allahu Taala* likes those who repent. In the third year of the Hegira, sane girls who had reached the age of puberty and women were ordered not to show themselves to unrelated (*na-mahram*) men. We should not believe the claim of the British spies and those ignorant people who have been trapped by them that, showing the unveiling before the revelation of the *ayat* about veiling (*hijab*) as evidence, the ordinance about veiling was fabricated later by scholars of *fiqh*.

One who says he or she is a Muslim has to know whether everything one does is compatible with Islam or not. If one does not know, then one has to learn by asking one of the scholars of *Ahl as-Sunna* or by reading their books. If what one does is not compatible with Islam, one will not escape from sin or disbelief. One has to repent truly every day. The sin or disbelief that is repented of will definitely be forgiven. If one does not repent, one will pay for it both in the world and in Hell. Such punishments are written in various parts of our book. The Muslim who commits a great sin will be taken out of Hell after being burned as much as the punishment for that sin is. Those who disbelieve *Allahu Taala* and disbelievers or *zindiq*s who try to destroy Islam will burn in Hell eternally.

Parts of the body that men and women are to cover during *salat* and at every place are called '***awrat***' (intimate, private) regions. It is *haram* to display one's private parts or to look at others' private parts. If one says that there is no concept with the name of *awrat* in Islam, one becomes a disbeliever. If a person says '*halal*' about or does not pay due importance to, that is does not fear of prescribed penalty (*adhab*) for, displaying or looking at a region which is *awrat* according to unanimity (*ijma*) of all the four *madhhab*s, that person becomes a disbeliever. As such is women's displaying their *awrat* regions or singing or reciting ***Mawlid*** among men. In the Hanbali *madhhab*, the region between the groins and the knees of the male body is not *awrat*.

One who says he or she is a Muslim has to learn and pay importance to the essentials of *iman* and *islam* in addition to those ordinances (*fard*s) and prohibitions (*haram*s) that were reported unanimously by the four *madhhab*s. Unknowing is not a valid excuse and is identical with disbelief despite knowing. The female bodily exterior, with the exception of her hands and face, is *awrat* according to all the four *madhhab*s. If one, because of not paying importance, exposes a region of one's body that is *awrat* without unanimity, that is not *awrat* in one of the other three *madhhab*s, one will not become a disbeliever but it is a great sin according to the *madhhab* one follows. An example of this is a man's exposing his thigh, the part between the groins and the knees. It is *fard* to learn what one does not know. As soon as one learns, one must repent and cover oneself.

Lying, gossip, backbiting, slander, theft, cheating, treachery, hurting someone's feelings, mischief-making, using someone's property without permission, not paying a laborer's or porter's due, rebellion, that is opposing the laws and the government's orders, and not paying taxes are sins, too. Committing them against disbelievers or in non-Muslim countries is *haram* as well. It is not disbelief (*kufr*) but sin (*fisq*) for non-educated people not to know the teachings that are not so wide-spread or indispensable for non-educated people to know.]

THE ESSENTIALS OF *IMAN*

"This noble person asked again, '**Oh! *Rasul-Allah*! Also tell me what *iman* is.**'" Having asked what was *islam* and the answer having been given, *Hadrat Jabrail* (*alayhis-salam*) asked our master *Rasulullah* (*sall-Allahu alayhi wa sallam*) to explain the reality and essence of *iman*. Literally *iman* means 'knowing a person to be perfectly truthful and having faith in them.' In Islam, *iman* means believing that *Rasulullah* (*sall-Allahu alayhi wa sallam*) is the Prophet (*an-Nạbi*) sent by *Allahu Taala*, knowing to be the truth and saying with belief that he is the Messenger chosen by *Allahu Taala*, believing in brief what he conveyed briefly and in detail what he conveyed in detail from *Allahu Taala*, and saying kalimat ash-shahada with the mouth whenever possible. Strong *iman* is such that, as we know for certain that fire burns and serpents kill by poisoning and so we try to avoid them, we should believe in *Allahu Taala* and His Attributes deeming them great, fully at heart, strive for His approval (*rida*), run to His Beauty (*Jamal*), escape from His wrath (*ghadab*) and from His torture (*adhab*), and place *iman* on the heart firmly like an inscription on marble.

Iman and *islam* conveyed by Muhammad (*alayhis-salam*) are the same. Belief in the meaning of *kalimat ash-shahada* is present in both of them. Although they differ in general and in particulars and have different literal meanings, there is no difference between them in Islam.

Is *iman* one thing or is it a combination of parts? If it is a combination, how many parts is it made of? Are Islamic practices (*amal, ibadat*, deeds) included in *iman* or not? While saying, "I have *iman*," is it right to add "**insha-*Allahu Taala***" (if *Allahu Taala* wills) or not? Is there littleness or muchness in *iman*? Is *iman* a creature? Is it within one's power to believe, or have the Believers believed under compulsion? If there is force or compulsion in believing, why was everybody commanded to believe? It would take a long time to explain all these one by one. Therefore, I will not answer them separately here. But it should be known that, according to the Ashari *madhhab* (see pp. 73 and 104) and the Mutazila (one of the 72 groups that deviated from *Ahl as-Sunna*), it is not probable (*jaiz*) for *Allahu Taala* to command us to do something that is not possible. According to the Mutazila, it is not probable for *Allahu Taala* to command something possible but which is not within human's power. According to the Ashari, however, it is probable yet *Allahu Taala* has not commanded it. To command people to fly in the air is of this sort. Neither in *iman* nor in rituals did *Allahu*

Taala command human creatures to do what they would not be able to do. For this reason, a person who, while a Muslim, goes mad or becomes *ghafil* (forgetful of *Allahu Taala*, unconscious) or sleeps and dies is still a Muslim, though not in a state of confirmation.

We should not think of the literal meaning of '*iman*' in this *hadith sharif* since even those who were uneducated in Arabia knew its literal meaning: 'confirmation, belief.' Certainly the *Sahabat al-Kiram* (*radiy-Allahu Taala anhum ajmain*) knew it, and *Jabrail* (*alayhis-salam*) wanted to teach the meaning of *iman* to them by asking *Rasulullah* (*sall-Allahu alayhi wa sallam*) what *iman* meant in Islam. '***Iman***' means to believe with heart and soul and to say with the mouth the six certain essentials by affirming through *kashf* (inspired unveiling of Divine mysteries) or *wijdan* (conscience), by understanding of the intellect out of an evidence, or by depending on and adapting a distinguished and approved statement. *Rasulullah* said that *iman* was to believe in six certain facts:

1– The first is to believe that ***Allahu Taala* is the Indispensable Being (*Wajib al-wujud*) and the Real Deity (Mabud) and the Creator of all creatures.** It should be believed for certain that He alone creates everything [every substance, atoms, elements, molecules, compounds, organic substances, cells, life, death, every event, every reaction, all kinds of power and sorts of energy, movements, laws, souls, angels and every being living or lifeless out of nothing, and He makes them all survive] in both this world and the next without material, time or similarity, out of nonexistence. As He created all creatures in the universe [in one moment while they had been nonexistent], He [creates some of them from one another and, when the Last Day comes, in one moment] will annihilate everything. He is the Creator, Owner and Absolute Ruler of all creatures. It has to be believed and acknowledged that there is nobody to dominate Him, to command Him or to be superior to Him. Every type of superiority and every attribute of perfection belong to Him only. No defect or no deficient attribute exists in Him. He is able to do what He wills. What He does is not intended to be useful to Himself or to others. He does not do anything for a reward. In everything He does, however, there are hidden causes (*hikma*), uses, blessings and favors.

Allahu Taala does not have to give what is good and useful for His human creatures, nor does He have to reward some people or punish some others. It would befit *Allahu Taala*'s superiority and benevolence if He would bring all the sinners to Paradise. It would become His justice if He would put all of those who obey and worship Him into Hell, yet He decreed and declared that He would put Muslims, those who worship Him, into Paradise and grant them favors, and that He would eternally torture disbelievers in Hell. He does not go back on His word. It would be of no use for Him if all the living creatures believed and worshipped Him, nor would it give Him any harm if all creatures became disbelievers, became excessive or disobeyed Him. If one wishes to do something, *Allahu Taala* creates it if He, too, wills it to be done. He alone is the One who creates every action of His human creatures and all things. If He does not will or create, nothing can move. If He does not wish, no one can become a disbeliever or a rebel. He lets disbelief and sins happen, yet He does not approve them. No one can interfere with His works. No one has the strength or the right to comment on how He must do anything or to ask the reason why He has done this or that. Excepting polytheism or disbelief that has been committed, He will forgive, if He wills, a person who dies without repenting for any great sin committed. *Allahu Taala* will punish them, if He wills, for a lesser sin. He declared that He would never forgive but torture eternally those who die as disbelievers and apostates.

Though *Allahu Taala* will torture in Hell those Muslims who, being ***Ahl al-qibla*** ('people of direction' who turn towards the Kaaba in ritual prayers), perform acts of worship yet whose beliefs (*itiqad, iman*) are not compatible with the beliefs of ***Ahl as-Sunna*** and who die without repenting, such Muslims, the **people of heresy (*ahl al-bida*),** will not remain in Hell eternally.

It is possible to see *Allahu Taala* with the eyes in this world, but no one ever has seen. At the Place of Gathering (*Mahshar*) on the Day of Judgment, He will be seen in His Wrath and Fury by disbelievers and sinful Muslims and in His Kindness and Beauty by pious Muslims. In Paradise, the Believers will see Him in His attribute Beauty. Angels and women, too, will see Him. Disbelievers will be deprived of this. There is a sound report conveying that genies also will be deprived of this. According to the majority of *ulama*, "Being honored with the manifestation of His Beauty (*tajalli al-Jamal*) and seeing (*ruyat*) Him will be every morning and every evening for Muslims whom *Allahu Taala* loves, every Friday for Muslims of low degree, and at a few times in a year such as times of festivals in this world for women."[1]

---

[1] *Hadrat* Shaikh Abd al-Haqq ad-Dahlawi (d. Delhi, 1642/1052) wrote in his Persian work ***Takmil al-iman***: "A *hadith sharif* states: '**You will see your Creator on the Day of Judgment as you see the [full] moon on the 14th [of the lunar month].**' As *Allahu Taala* is known incomprehensibly in this world, *Allahu Taala* will be seen

It should be believed that *Allahu Taala* will be seen, yet we should not think of how He will be seen since His works cannot be comprehended through intellect. They do not resemble worldly matters. [They cannot be evaluated with physical or chemical criteria.] Such concepts as aspect or being across have no connection with Him. He is not material. He is not an object [nor is He an element, an alloy or a compound]. He is not countable, measurable or computable. No change happens in Him. He is not located at a place. He is not with time. He does not have a past or a future, front or back, bottom or top, nor right or left. Therefore, human reasoning, knowledge or intellect cannot comprehend anything of Him. So, humans cannot comprehend how He will be seen. Although such words as hand, foot, direction, place and the like, which are not suitable for *Allahu Taala*, exist in *ayat*s and *hadith*s, they are not used in the sense that we know and use today. Such *ayat*s and *hadith*s are called ***mutashabihat*** (those with incomprehensible, hidden meanings). We have to believe them, but we should not attempt to understand what or how they are. Or their ***tawil*** (interpreting suitably with Islam) can be made briefly or in detail; that is they can be given meanings suitable for *Allahu Taala*. For example, the word 'hand' may be interpreted as power or energy.

Muhammad (*alayhis-salam*) saw *Allahu Taala* during the *Miraj*. But this seeing was not with the eyes, like seeing in this world. One who says that one has seen Him in this world is a *zindiq*. The seeing experienced by the *awliya* (*qaddas-Allahu Taala asrarahum ajmain*: may *Allahu Taala* make all their mystiques decent, sacred and blessed!) was unlike seeing in this world or seeing in the next world.

---

incomprehensibly in the hereafter. Great scholars such as Abul-Hasan al-Ashari, *Al-Imam* as-Suyuti and *Al-Imam* al-Bayhaki said that also *angels* were going to see *Allahu Taala* in Paradise. *Al-Imam al-Azam* Abu Hanifa and some other scholars said that genies did not earn *thawab* and would not enter Paradise and that only faithful genies would escape Hell. Women will see *Allahu Taala* a few times in a year such as times of festivals in this world. Perfect (*kamil*) Believers will see Him every morning and evening while others will see Him on Fridays. To this humble person myself, this good news covers the faithful women and angels and genies, too; it would be proper that the perfect and *arif* women such as Fatimat az-Zahra, Khadijat al-Kubra, Aishat as-Siddiqa and other Decent Wives [of the Prophet] and *Hadrat* Mariam (the Virgin Mary) and *Hadrat* Asiya be given special treatment. *Al-Imam* as-Suyuti, too, meant this."

In other words, what they experienced was not ***ruyat*** (seeing) but ***shuhud*** (seeing the examples/*mithal*s through the 'eyes' of their hearts).

Some great *awliya* said that they had seen Him, yet they mistook the *shuhud* they experienced while they were unconscious (*sakr*) for *ruyat.* Or this is one of their words that are to be understood by *tawil.*

> **Question:** "It is said above that it is possible (*jaiz*) to see *Allahu Taala* with the eyes in this world. Then why should a person who says something which is possible to happen be a *zindiq*? If a person who says so becomes a disbeliever, can it be said to be possible?"

Answer: The literal meaning of ' *jaiz* ' is 'possible to happen or not.' However, according to the *madhhab* of al-Ashari [Abul-Hasan Ali ibn Ismail, d. Baghdad, 941/330], the possibility of *ruyat* means that, unlike being close to or facing Him or seeing through the physical laws He created in this world, *Allahu Taala* is capable of creating in humans quite a different sense for seeing. For example, He is able, so it is possible, to show a mosquito in Andalusia (southern Spain) to a blind person in China, and anything on the moon or on a star to a human on the earth. Such power is peculiar to Him only. Secondly, saying, "I saw *Allahu Taala* in this world," is incompatible with the *Quran al-Karim* and with the consensus of the scholars (*ulama*). Therefore, those who make such a statement are ***mulhid*s** or ***zindiq*s**.[1] As the third answer, the statement, "It is possible to see *Allahu Taala* in this world," does not mean, "It is possible to see Him on the earth within the physical laws." However, one who says one saw Him means that one saw Him as one sees other things; this is a seeing which is not possible. A person who makes such statements that cause disbelief is called a *mulhid* or a *zindiq.* [After these answers, *Hadrat* Mawlana Khalid wrote, "Be careful!" thus he directed attention to the second answer that was more sound.]

Elapse of time, day or night, cannot be related to *Allahu Taala.* Since there can be no change in Him in any respect, it cannot be said that He was in this manner in the past or He will be like that in the

---

[1] ***Mulhid*s** or ***zindiq*s** say that they are Muslims. *Mulhid*s are sincere in their word; they believe that they are Muslims on the right path. However, *zindiq*s are enemies of Islam who make themselves appear to be Muslims in order to harm Islam from within and to deceive Muslims.

future. He does not penetrate (*hulul*) into anything.[1] He does not unite with anything. He never has an opposite, the like, partner, assistant or protector. He does not have a father, mother, son, daughter or spouse. He is always present with everybody, surrounds and overlooks everything. To everyone He is closer than his main blood vessel. However, His presence, togetherness, closeness or surrounding us is not like what we understand. His closeness cannot be comprehended with the knowledge of scholars, with the intellect of scientists or with the *kashf* or *shuhud* of *awliya* (qaddas-*Allahu Taala asrarahum ajmain*). Human reason cannot understand their inner meanings. *Allahu Taala* is unique in *adh-Dhat* (Self, Personality) and *as-Sifat* (Attributes). No change or differentiation takes place in any of them.

Allahu Taala's names are ***tawqifi***, that is only the names shown by Islam are permitted to be used, and it is not permissible to use other words.[2]

His names are infinite. It is well-known that He has 1001 names; that is He revealed 1001 of them to humanity. In the religion of Muhammad (*alayhis-salam*), 99 of them called '***al-Asma al-Husna***' (the Beautiful Names) were revealed.

The ***Sifat adh-Dhatiyya*** (Personal Attributes) of *Allahu Taala* are six (see p. 19). *The* ***Sifat ath-Thubutiyya*** (those Divine Attributes partially exemplified in creatures, see p. 21 and below) of *Allahu Taala* are eight according to the ***Maturidiyya*** *madhhab* and seven in the ***Ashariyya*** *madhhab* (see pp. 73 and 104); like His Dhat, these [latter] attributes of *Allahu Taala* were eternal in the past and are everlasting, that is they, too, exist eternally. They are sacred. They are not like the attributes of creatures. They cannot be comprehended through reasoning or assumption or by comparing them with beings in the world. He has endowed human beings with

---

[1] Those Shiites who belong to the group called '**Nusayri**' believe that *Allahu Taala* has penetrated *Hadrat* Ali. This wrong belief causes them to become disbelievers.

[2] For instance, *Allahu Taala* may be called '*Alîm*' (the 'Omniscient'), but we cannot use '*faqih*' which also means '*âlim*' (scholar, one trained in Islamic sciences), for Islam does not use '*faqih*' for *Allahu Taala*. Similarly, it is not permissible to say 'God' instead of Allah, because 'god' means 'idol' or 'deity'; "Ox is the god of Hindus," is said, for instance. It is permissible to say, "Allah is One; there is no god but He." Words like Dieu (French), Gott (German) and God can be used for idol or deity, but not for Allah.

an example of each of these attributes. Seeing these examples, His Attributes can be understood to some extent. Since humans cannot comprehend Him, it is not permissible to think of or to attempt to comprehend Him. The eight attributes of His are neither the same as nor other than His Dhat; that is His Attributes do not make up His Dhat, nor are they other than Himself. These eight Attributes are:

Hayat (Life), ***Ilm*** (Omniscience), ***Sam*** (Hearing), ***Basar*** (Seeing), ***Qudra*** (Omnipotence), ***Kalam*** (Speech, Word), ***Irada*** (Will), and ***Takwin*** (Creativeness). In the *Ashariyya madhhab, Takwin* and *Qudra* make up the same attribute. *Mashiyya* is synonymous with *Irada.*

Each of the eight attributes of *Allahu Taala* is plain and is in a single phase. No change occurs in any of them, yet each of them is various in respect of its relation to creatures. That an attribute of His is multiple in its relation to or affecting the creatures does not harm its being plain. Similarly, even though He has created so many kinds of creatures and is protecting all of them against annihilation every moment, He is still One. No change ever occurs in Him. Every creature needs Him every moment in every respect. He does not need anybody.

2– The second of the six essentials to believe is "**belief in *Allahu Taala*'s angels**." '*Malak'* (angel) means 'envoy', 'messenger' or 'power'. Angels are material but ethereal (*latif*), more ethereal than the gaseous phase of matter. They are *nurani* (luminous, radiant, spiritual). They are alive. They have intellect (*aql*). Evils of human beings do not exist in angels. They can take any shape. As gases turn into liquid and solid and take a shape when becoming solid, angels can form beautiful shapes. Angels are not souls that have parted from bodies of great people. Christians presume that angels are such souls. Unlike energy or power, they are not immaterial. Some ancient philosophers supposed them to be immaterial. All of them are called '***malaika***'. Angels were created before all other living creatures. Therefore, we were commanded to believe in them before believing in the heavenly books, which come before belief in the prophets; and in the *Quran al-Karim* the names of these beliefs are given in this succession.

Belief in angels has to be as follows: angels are creatures of *Allahu Taala.* They are not His partners, nor are they His daughters as disbelievers and polytheists supposed. He loves all angels. They obey His commands and never commit sins or disobey the commands. They are neither male nor female. They do not get married. They do not have children. They are alive. Although a statement referred to *Hadrat* Abdullah ibn Masud (*radiy-Allahu anh*) said that some angels had had children among which the Satan and genies had been counted, it is responded in books in detail. When *Allahu Taala* announced that He was going to create human beings, angels asked, "**Oh** [*Allahu Taala*]**! Are You going to create the creatures who will cause chaos and shed blood over the world?**" Such questions, called '***zalla***', of angels do not change the fact that they are innocent.

Of all creatures, angels are the most numerous. No one but *Allahu Taala* knows their number. There is no empty space in the skies where angels do not worship. Every place in the skies is occupied by angels in *ruku* (bowing during *salat*) or in *sajda* (prostrating). In the skies, on the earth, in grass, on stars, in every living and lifeless creature, in every rain-drop, plant-leaf, atom, molecule, in every reaction, motion and in everything, angels have duties. They carry out *Allahu Taala*'s commands everywhere. They are intermediaries between Him and creatures. Some of them are the superiors of other angels. Some of them brought messages to the prophets (*alayhimus-salam*, 'May peace be upon them'). Some angels bring good thoughts to the human heart, which is called '***ilham***' (inspiration). Some others have lost consciousness upon facing *Allahu Taala*'s Beauty and are unaware of all human beings and creatures. Each of these angels stays in a certain place and cannot leave its place. Some angels have two wings and some have four or more.[1] Angels belonging to Paradise stay in Paradise. Their superior is ***Ridwan***. Angels of Hell, ***Zabani***s, carry out in Hell what they are commanded. The fire of Hell does not harm them, as the sea is not harmful to fish. There are nineteen leading *Zabani*s. Their chief is ***Malik***.

For each human being, there are four angels who record all their good and bad deeds. Two of them come at night and the other two

---

[1] As the wings of each kind of birds and those of an airplane are of their own structure and are different from the wings of one another, angels' wings have their own structure. When we hear the name of something which we have not seen or do not know, we are mistaken by guessing that it is like the things we know. We believe that angels have wings, but we do not know how they are. Pictures of winged women in churches, publications or movies, which are regarded as angels, are all false. Muslims do not make such pictures. We should not regard these unrealistic pictures drawn by non-Muslims to be true, and we should not believe the adversaries.

come during the day. They are called '***kiraman katibin***' (incorruptible recorders) or '***hafaza***' (record-keeping) angels. According to another report, *hafaza* angels are different from *kiraman katibin.* The angel on one's right side is superior to the one on the left and records the good deeds. The one on the left writes down the evil deeds. There are angels who will torture disbelievers and disobedient Muslims in their graves, and those who will ask questions in graves. The questioning angels are called '***munkar***' and '***nakir***'. Angels who will question Muslims are also called '***mubashshir***' and '***bashir***' (good news givers).

Angels have superiority to one another. The most superior angels are the four archangels. The first of them is ***Jabrail*** (*alayhis-salam*). *Jabrail*'s duty was to bring divine revelation (***wahy***) to the prophets, to inform them of the commands and prohibitions. The second one is ***Israfil*** (*alayhis-salam*), who will sound the last trump called '***Sur***'. *Israfil* will sound the *Sur* twice. Excepting *Allahu Taala*, every living being will die at the first sound. At the second sound all will be brought back to life. The third one is ***Mikail*** (*alayhis-salam*). It is his duty to make up cheapness, expensiveness, scarcity, abundance [economic order, bringing comfort and ease] and to move every object. The fourth one is ***Azrail*** (*alayhis-salam*) who takes souls (Persian '*jan*' and Arabic '*ruh*') from human bodies. After these four, there are four superior classes of angels: four angels of ***Hamalat al-Arsh***, who will be eight on the Day of Resurrection; angels in the Divine Presence, called '***muqarrabun***'; leaders of torturing angels, called '***karubiyun***'; and angels of Mercy, named '***ruhaniyun***'. All these higher angels are also higher than all human beings except the prophets (*alayhimus-salawatu wat-taslimat*). The *sulaha* (the pious avoiding sinning) and *awliya* (plural of *wali*, one loved by *Allahu Taala*) among Muslims are higher than common or lower angels. And common angels are superior to common Muslims, that is disobedient, sinful ones. Disbelievers, however, are lower than all creatures.

At the first sound of the *Sur*, all angels except *Hamalat al-Arsh* and the four archangels will be annihilated. Then the *Hamalat al-Arsh* and then the four archangels will be annihilated. At the second sound all angels will come back to life. The *Hamalat al-Arsh* and the four archangels will rise before the second sound of the Sur. That is these angels will be annihilated after all the living creatures, as they were created before all.

3. "**Believing the books revealed by *Allahu Taala***" is the third of the six essentials of *iman.* He sent these books to some prophets by

making the angel read to them. To some He sent books inscribed on tablets, and to some others He made them hear without the angel in between. All these books are the Word of Allah (*Kalam-Allah*). They are eternal in the past and everlasting. They are not creatures. They are not words made up by angels, nor are they words of the prophets. The Word of *Allahu Taala* is unlike the language which we write, keep in mind and speak. It is not like presence in writing, speech or mind. It does not have letters or sounds. Humans cannot understand how He and His Attributes are, but they can read that Word, keep it in mind and write it. It becomes *hâdith* (that created later) when it is with us. When it is with human beings, it is *hâdith* and a creature. When it is thought as the Word of *Allahu Taala*, it is eternal from the beginning (*qadim*).

All the Books sent by *Allahu Taala* are genuine and correct. There is no lie or error in them. It was stated that it was possible for Him to forgive despite His declaration that He will punish and torture; this might be because this forgiveness is conditional on situations beyond our knowledge, or on His Own Will and Choice. Or it is meant to express that He will forgive the penalty that humans deserve. Since the declaration about punishment and torture does not narrate an event, it cannot be a lie when He forgives. Although *Allahu Taala*'s not giving the gifts promised is not probable, *Allahu Taala*'s forgiving penalties is possible. Both intellect and *ayat*s disclosed that this was so.

It is necessary to explain *ayat*s and *hadith*s in their usual meanings, unless there is an obstacle or an inconvenience. It is not permissible to give other meanings similar to these meanings.[1] Ayats called ***mutashabihat*** have incomprehensible, hidden meanings. Only *Allahu Taala* knows and very few distinguished superiors who have been granted *al-ilm al-ladunni* (knowledge inspired by *Allahu Taala* to the hearts of *awliya*) can understand their meanings as far as they have been allowed. No one else can understand them. For this reason, we should believe that *ayat*s of *mutashabihat* are of the Word of *Allahu Taala*, and we should not investigate their meanings. Scholars of the *Ashari madhhab* said that brief or detailed *tawil* of such *ayat*s were permitted. '***Tawil***'

---

[1] The *Quran al-Karim* and the *Hadith ash-Sharif* are in the *Quraysh* (an Arab tribe to which Muhammad *alayhis-salam* belonged) language and dialect, and the words should be given the meanings used in the *Hijaz* (the region on the Arabian Peninsula on the Red Sea coast where Mecca and Medina are situated) 1400 years ago. It is not correct to translate them by giving them today's meanings, which are the results of changes throughout centuries.

means ‘choosing, from among several meanings of a word, the one which is not common.’ For example, about the *ayat*, “**The Hand of Allah is superior to theirs,**” which is the Word of *Allahu Taala*, we should say, “I believe whatever *Allahu Taala* meant by this.” It is the best to say, “I cannot understand its meaning. Only *Allahu Taala* knows.” Or we must say, “*Allahu Taala*’s knowledge is unlike our knowledge. His Will is not like our will. Similarly, His Hand is not like the hands of human creatures.”

In the Books revealed by *Allahu Taala*, either the pronunciations or the meanings of some *ayat*s, or both, were changed (***naskh***) by Him. The *Quran al-Karim* replaced all the Books and abolished the validity of the rules in them. There will never be any mistakes, additions, forgotten or missing parts in the *Quran al-Karim* until the end of the world. All knowledge of the past and the future exists in the *Quran al-Karim*. For this reason, it is higher and more valuable than all the Books. The greatest *mujiza* (miracle created by *Allahu Taala* through a prophet) of *Rasulullah* (*sall-Allahu Taala alayhi wa sallam*) is the *Quran al-Karim*. If all human beings and genies came together and tried to say something similar to the shortest *sura* of the *Quran al-Karim*, they would not be able to say. In fact, the eloquent, literary poets of Arabia assembled and strove very hard, but they were not able to say something like one short *ayat*. They could not stand against the *Quran al-Karim*. They were stupefied. *Allahu Taala* makes the enemies of Islam incapable and defeated before the *Quran al-Karim*. The eloquence of the *Quran al-Karim* is above human power. Human beings are incapable of saying as it says. *Ayats* in the *Quran al-Karim* are unlike the poetry, prose or rhymed verse of human beings. Nevertheless, it was said in the letters of the language spoken by the literary, eloquent people of Arabia.

The number of heavenly Books revealed to humanity is 104: it is well-known that 10 ***suhuf*** (pl. of *sahifa*, booklet) were revealed to **Adam**, 50 *suhuf* to **Shis** (**Sheth**), 30 *suhuf* to **Idris** and 10 *suhuf* to **Ibrahim** (**Abraham**); the ***Tawrat*** (the ***Torah***) was revealed to **Musa** (**Moses**), the ***Zabur (Psalms)*** to **Dawud** (**David**), the ***Injil*** (Latin ‘***Evangelium*’**, the original of the New Testament) to **Isa** (**Jesus**) and the ***Quran al-Karim*** (the Gracious ***Koran)*** to **Muhammad** (*alayhimus-salam*).

When one wants to order or forbid something, to ask something or to give some news, first one thinks about and prepares it in one’s mind. Such meanings in mind are called “***kalam nafsi***,” which cannot be said to be Arabic, Persian or English. Their being expressed in various languages does not cause these meanings to change. Words expressing these meanings are called "***kalam lafzi.***" *Kalam lafzi* can be expressed in different languages. So, *kalam nafsi* of a person is a pure, unchangeable, distinct attribute that exists in its possessor like other attributes such as knowledge, will, discernment, etc, and *kalam lafzi* is a group of letters that express *kalam nafsi*, come out of the mouth of the person uttering them and reach the ear. Similarly, the Word of *Allahu Taala* is the eternal-in-the-past, everlasting, non-silent, non-created Word existent with His Person. It is an Attribute distinct from the *Sifat adh-Dhatiyya* and from *the Sifat ath-Thubutiyya* of *Allahu Taala*, such as Knowledge and Will.

The Attribute *Kalam* (Speech, Word) never changes and is pure. It is not in letters or sounds. It cannot be categorized or classified as a command, a prohibition, a narration or as Arabic, Persian, Hebrew, Turkish or Syriac (Assyrian). It does not take such forms. It cannot be written. It does not need such apparatuses or media as intelligence, ear or tongue. It can be told in any language wished. So, if it is expressed in Arabic it is called the *Quran al-Karim*. If it is expressed in Hebrew it is the *Tawrat*. If it is expressed in Syriac it is the *Injil*.[1]

The Word of *Allahu Taala* (*Kalam al-ilahiyya*) tells various subjects; if it narrates the events that happened or that will happen, it is called ***khabar*** (narration); if not so, it is called ***insha***. If it states things that should be done, it is called ***amr*** (command). If it states forbidden things, it is ***nahy*** (prohibition). But no change or increase occurs in the Word of *Allahu Taala*. All books and booklets revealed are from the Attribute *Kalam* of *Allahu Taala*; that is they are of His ***Kalam an-Nafsi***, and its Arabic is the *Quran al-Karim*. The Divine revelation (*wahy)* sent in statements that can be written in the form of letters and can be said, heard and kept in mind is called the ***Kalam al-Lafzi*** or the ***Quran al-Karim***. Since the *Kalam al-Lafzi* denotes the *Kalam an-Nafsi*, it is permissible to call it the *Kalam al-ilahiyya* or the Divine Attribute. As the whole of it is called the *Quran al-Karim*, its parts are also called the *Quran al-Karim*.

Scholars of the right way unanimously say that the *Kalam an-Nafsi* is not a creature and that it is *qadim* (eternal in the past, pre-eternal). There is no unanimity on whether the *Kalam al-Lafzi* is created or pre-eternal. Some who regarded the *Kalam al-Lafzi* as

---

[1] It is written in the book entitled ***Sharh al-maqasid*** (by Saduddin Taftazani, d. Samarkand, 1389/792) that its expression in Greek is the *Injil*, and its expression in Syriac is the *Zabur*.

created warned that it would be better not to say that it is created, because if said so, it would come to mean that the *Kalam an-Nafsi* is a creature. This is the best remark about the matter. When the human mind hears something that denotes something else, it simultaneously remembers the denoted thing. Those scholars among *Ahl as-Sunna* who said that the *Quran al-Karim* was created meant the sounds and words we utter with our mouth. The scholars of *Ahl as-Sunna* have unanimously stated that both the *Kalam an-Nafsi* and the *Kalam al-Lafzi* are the Word of Allah. Although some scholars considered this statement metaphoric, the *Kalam an-Nafsi*'s being the Word of Allah means that it is His Attribute of Speech, and the *Kalam* al-Lafzi's being the Word of *Allahu Taala* means that He is its Creator.

> **Question**: "From the writing above it is understood that the pre-eternal Word of *Allahu Taala* cannot be heard. Saying, 'I have heard the Word of Allah,' means 'I have heard the sounds and words uttered,' or 'I understood the sound voiced and the pre-eternal *Kalam an-Nafsi.*' All the prophets could and, even everybody, can hear it in both of these two manners. What is the reason for distinguishing Musa (*alayhis-salam*) as ***Kalim-Allah*** (one to whom *Allahu Taala* spoke)?"

Answer: Musa (*alayhis-salam*) heard the Pre-eternal Word without letters or sounds, in a way different from the Divine Custom (*al-Adat al-Ilahiyya*). He heard it in a manner that cannot be explained, as *Allahu Taala* will be seen in Paradise in an unintelligible, unexplainable manner. Nobody else heard it in this manner. Or, he heard the Word of Allah in sounds not only through his ears but also through every particle of his body, from every direction. Or, he heard it only from the direction of the tree, yet not in sounds or with the vibration of air or with other means. Because he heard it in one of these three ways, he was honored with the name '*Kalim-Allah*'. Muhammad (*alayhis-salam*) also heard the Divine Word in this manner during the *Miraj*. So *was Jabrail's (alayhis-salam)* hearing as he received *wahy*.

4. The fourth of the six essentials of *iman* is "**to believe in the prophets sent by *Allahu Taala*,**" to guide to and make people attain the right way He likes. Literally, '*rusul*' (pl. of *rasul*) were the 'people sent, messengers.' In Islam, '***rasul***' means 'noble, respectable person whose nature, character, knowledge and intellect were higher than those of all the people of his time, and who did not have even a single bad trait in his character and no disliked manner.' The prophets had the quality ***isma***; that is they did

not commit any great or small sins before or after they were informed of their *nubuwwa* (the prophetship, prophethood).[1] After they were informed of their prophetship and until their prophetship was known and spread, they did not have such disabilities as blindness, deafness or the like. It has to be believed that every prophet had seven peculiarities: ***amana*** (trustworthiness), ***sidq*** (devotion), ***tabligh*** (calling people to, and conveying, commands and prohibitions of *Allahu Taala*'s religion), ***adala*** (justness), ***isma*** (protection against sinning), ***fatana*** (superintelligence) and ***amn al-azl*** (security against dismissal from *nubuwwa*).

The prophet who brought a new religion (system of ritual rules) is called "***rasul***", and one who did not bring a new religion but invited people to the previous one is called "***nabi***".[2] In conveying commands and calling people to *Allahu Taala*'s religion, there is no difference between them. Belief in the prophets means believing, without discrimination, that all of them were devoted and truthful. One who disbelieves one of them is regarded as having disbelieved all of them. Prophethood cannot be attained by working hard, by suffering hunger or discomfort or by worshipping much. It is assigned only by *Allahu Taala*'s favor and selection. Heavenly religions were sent through the mediation of the prophets in order to arrange a useful life for humanity in this world and the next and to prevent them from harmful acts and make them attain deliverance, guidance and peace. Although they had many enemies and were mocked and treated harshly, the prophets did not fear the enemies and showed no hesitation in propagating *Allahu Taala*'s commands about beliefs and practices among people. *Allahu Taala* supported the prophets with miracles (*mujiza*s) to show that they were devoted and truthful. No one could challenge their miracles. People who follow a certain prophet is called his '***umma***'. On the Day of Judgment, the prophets will be permitted to intercede for their *umma*s, especially for the ones who would be gravely sinful, and their intercession will be accepted. *Allahu Taala* will also permit the *ulama*, *sulaha* and *awliya* among their *umma*s to intercede, and their intercession will be accepted. The prophets (*alayhimus-salawatu wat-taslimat*) are alive in their graves in a life

---

[1] Some disbelievers who insidiously try to destroy Islam say, "Before becoming the Prophet, Muhammad [*alayhis-salam*] had offered sacrificial animals to idols," and give reference to *la-madhhabi* books as documents. The lines above prove that this assertion is a lie.

[2] 'prophet' and 'messenger' are used for both.

we cannot know; earth does not cause their blessed bodies to decompose. For this reason, it was stated in a *hadith sharif*: **"The prophets perform *salat* and *hajj* in their graves."**[1]

As the blessed eyes of a prophet slept, the eyes of his heart did not sleep. All the prophets (*alayhimus-salam*) were equal in doing their duties as the prophets and in possessing the perfections of the prophetship. The above-mentioned seven peculiarities existed in all the prophets. The prophets were never dismissed from *nubuwwa*. *Awliya*, however, may be deprived of *wilaya* (the state of being a *wali*, one loved by *Allahu Taala*). The prophets were human beings, not genies or angels that could never be the prophets for human beings or attain the degree of a prophet. The prophets had superiority to and honors above one another. For example, in respect to having superiorities such as the numerousness of believers in his *umma*, extent of the countries whereon he was designated, being widespread of his knowledge and *marifa* (knowledge about *Allahu Taala*), his miracles' being numerous and continuous and his being endowed with exclusive values and blessings, the Prophet of this, the latest, age, **Muhammad** (*alayhis-salam*), was higher than all other prophets. The prophets called '***Ulul-azm***' were higher than others. *Rasul*s were higher than *nabi*s who were not *rasul*s.

The number of the prophets (*alayhimus-salam*) is not known. It is widely known that there were more than 124,000. Of them, 313 or 315 were *rasul*s; the six higher *rasul*s among them, called '***Ulul-azm***',

---

[1] Today, the people called '***Wahhabis***' in Arabia do not believe such *hadith*s. They claim that the true Muslims who believe them are disbelievers. By misinterpreting those *ayat*s and *hadith*s with unclear, ambiguous meanings, they become people of ***bida*** but not disbelievers. They greatly harm Muslims. Wahhabism was founded by a fool named Muhammad ibn Abd al-Wahhab of the Najd region, Arabia. Hempher, a British spy, misled him by using the heretical ideas of Ahmad ibn Taymiyya (d. Damascus, 1328/728). It spread among the Turks and everywhere through the books of an Egyptian named Muhammad Abduh (d. Egypt, 1905/1323). Scholars of *Ahl as-Sunna* proved in hundreds of their books that Wahhabism was not a fifth *madhhab* and that *Wahhabis* were heretical (*dalala*) people following a wrong way. Detailed information is provided in ***Endless Bliss***, in ***Confessions of a British Spy*** and in ***Advice for the Muslim***. May *Allahu Taala* protect young professionals of the Religion from falling into Wahhabism, which was established by the British! May *Allahu Taala* not let us deviate from the way of scholars of *Ahl as-Sunna*, who were praised in many *hadith*s!

were: **Adam**, **Nuh** (Noah), **Ibrahim** (Abraham), **Musa** (Moses), **Isa** (Jesus) and **Muhammad** Mustafa (*alayhimus-salam*).

The following 33 prophets are well-known: **Adam, Idris** (Enoch), **Sheth** (Shis), **Nuh** (Noah), **Hud** (Heber), **Salih** (Methusaleh), **Ibrahim** (Abraham), **Lut** (Lot), **Ismail** (Ishmael), **Ishaq** (Isaac), **Yaqub** (Jacob), **Yusuf** (Joseph), **Ayyub** (Job), **Shuayb** (Jethro), **Musa** (Moses), **Harun** (Aaron), **Khidir, Yusha ibn Nun** (Joshua), **Ilyas** (Elias), **Alyasa** (Elisha), **Dhul-kifl** (Ezekiel), **Shamun, Ishmoil** (Ismail), **Yunus ibn Mata** (Jonah), **Dawud** (David), Sulaiman (Solomon), **Luqman, Zakariyya** (Zachariah), **Yahya** (John the Baptist), **Uzayr** (Ezra), **Isa** (Jesus) **ibn Mariam, Dhul-qarnayn** (Zulqarnayn) and **Muhammad** (*alayhimus-salam*).

The names of only 28 of them are written in the *Quran al-Karim.* Sheth, Khidir, Yusha, Shamun and Ishmoil are not written. It is not certain whether Dhul-qarnayn, Luqman and Uzayr were the prophets or not. As written in the 36th letter of the second volume of ***Maktubat-i Mathumiyya*** of M. Mathum, the reports stating that Khidir (*alayhis-salam*) had been a prophet were authentic, and in the 182nd letter, he wrote, "Khidir's (*alayhis-salam*) appearing in a human form and doing certain things do not show that he is alive. *Allahu Taala* has given Khidir's soul, as well as the souls of many other prophets and *wali*s, the permission to appear in a human form. Seeing them does not show that they are alive." Dhul-kifl (*alayhis-salam*) was also called 'Harqil', who was also said to be Ilyas, Idris or Zakariyya.

Ibrahim (*alayhis-salam*) was *Khalil-Allah* (Adorer to Allah) because, having no love for creatures, there was only love for *Allahu Taala* in his heart. Musa (*alayhis-salam*) was *Kalim-Allah* because he spoke with *Allahu Taala.* Isa (*alayhis-salam*) was *Kalimat-Allah* because he did not have a father and was born only upon the Divine Word (*al-Kalimat al-Ilahiyya*) 'Be!' Furthermore, he conveyed *Allahu Taala*'s words that were full of Divine Wisdom to the ears of people through preaching.

Muhammad (*alayhis-salam*), who was the reason for the creation of all creatures and is the highest, the most prominent, the most honorable of humankind, is *Habib-Allah* (*Allahu Taala*'s Dearest/Beloved). There were many evidences proving his greatness and superiority and that he was *Habib-Allah.* For this reason, such words as 'was overcome' or 'was defeated' cannot be said about him. On the Day of the Resurrection, he will rise from his grave before everybody. He will be first to go to the place of Judgment. He will go to Paradise before everybody. Although his miracles are countless and human power cannot suffice to count them, we will ornament our writings by narrating the miracle of the *Miraj*:

While *Rasulullah* (*alayhis-salam*) was in bed in *al-Makkat al-Mukarrama* (Mecca), he was awakened and his blessed body was taken to the ***Aqsa* Mosque** in Jerusalem (***Quds***), then to the skies and, after the seventh sky, to the places which *Allahu Taala* determined. We have to believe in the *Miraj* in this manner.[1] He and *Jabrail* (*alayhimas-salam*) went from Mecca to ***Sidrat al-muntaha***, a tree in the sixth and seventh skies. No knowledge, no ascent could go further than there. In Sidra, *Rasulullah* saw *Jabrail* (*alayhimas-salam*) in his own shape with his six hundred wings. *Jabrail* (*alayhis-salam*) remained in Sidra. From Mecca to Jerusalem, or to the seventh sky, *Rasulullah* (*alayhis-salam*) was taken on ***Buraq***, which was a white, very fast, genderless and unworldly animal of Paradise, smaller than a mule and bigger than an ass. It stepped beyond eyeshot. At the *Aqsa* Mosque, *Rasulullah* and other prophets (*alayhimus-salam*) performed *salat* in *jamaa*, *Rasulullah* conducting the *salat* as the *imam*; it was dusk (*isha*) or dawn (*fajr*) prayer. The prophets' souls were present there in their own human figures. From Jerusalem up to the seventh sky, he was made to ascend with an unknown ladder named ***Miraj*** in a moment. On the way, angels lined up on the right and on the left, praised and lauded him. At each sky, *Jabrail* (*alayhis-salam*) announced the good news of *Rasulullah*'s (*alayhis-salam*) arrival. In each sky he saw a prophet and greeted him. In Sidra, he saw many astonishing things, the blessings in Paradise and the tortures in Hell. He looked at none of the blessings of Paradise out of the desire for and the pleasure of seeing *Allahu Taala*'s Beauty (*Jamal*). Beyond *Sidra*, he went ahead alone, among *nurs* (radiance). He heard the sounds of angels' pens. He passed through 70 000 curtains. The distance between two curtains was like a way of 500 years. Then, on a bed named ***Rafraf*** which was brighter than the sun, he passed through the ***Kursi*** (part of the skies outside the seventh sky and inside the ***Arsh***, which is the end of matter bordering the skies) and reached the Divine Arsh. He went beyond the Arsh, beyond the worlds of

---

[1] The Ismaili heretics and the enemies of Islam disguised as Islamic scholars try to deceive the youth by saying and writing that the *Miraj* was not a bodily ascent but a spiritual state *(hal)*. We should not buy such corrupt books; we should not let them deceive us. How the *Miraj* happened is written in detail in many valuable books, for example in ***Shifa-i sharif*** by Qadi Iyad al-Maliki (d. Morocco in 1150/544) and ***Endless Bliss***.

time, space and matter. He reached the position where he could hear *Allahu Taala*'s speech.

He saw *Allahu Taala* in a manner that cannot be understood or explained, just as *Allahu Taala* will be seen in the hereafter without time and space. He spoke with *Allahu Taala* without letters and sounds. He glorified, praised and lauded *Allahu Taala*. He was given innumerable gifts and honors. He and his *umma* (community of believers of a prophet) were commanded to perform *salat* fifty times daily, but it was gradually reduced to five times with the mediation of Musa (*alayhis-salam*). Before that, *salat* had been performed only in the mornings and in the afternoons or at nights. After such a long journey, having attained gifts and blessings and having seen and heard so many bewildering things, he was back to his bed, which was still warm. What we have written above was understood partly from *ayat*s and partly from *hadith*s. Though it is not obligatory (*wajib*) to believe all, people who disbelieve these reports will be separated from the *Ahl as-Sunna* since the scholars of *Ahl as-Sunna* conveyed them. Those who do not believe an *ayat* or *hadith*s become disbelievers.

Let us cite some of the innumerable evidences showing that Muhammad (*alayhis-salam*) is the Most Superior of the prophets (***Sayyid al-Anbiya***):

On the Day of Judgement all the prophets will shelter in the shade of his flag. *Allahu Taala* had ordered all the prophets (*alayhimus-salam*) that, if they had remained alive till the time of Muhammad (*alayhis-salam*) who, among creatures, had been *Allahu Taala*'s Beloved Elect, they would have believed and helped him. Also, all the prophets had ordered their *umma*s the same in their last requests.

Muhammad (*alayhis-salam*) was the Last Prophet (***Khatam al-Anbiya***); that is no prophet will succeed him. His blessed soul was created before all the prophets. The rank of the prophetship was given first to him. The prophetship was completed with his honoring the world. Towards the end of the world, during the time of *Hadrat* al-Mahdi, Isa (*alayhis-salam*) will descend from heaven to Damascus and join Muhammad's (*alayhis-salam*) *umma* and spread Islam on the earth.

> [The heretical people called '***Qadianis***' or '***Ahmadis***' who were organized by the British in India in 1880/1296, tell slanderous lies about Isa (*alayhis-salam*), too. Although they claim to be Muslims, they strive to destroy Islam from within. A *fatwa* (ruling made on a religious matter by Islamic

scholars) was issued to declare that they were not Muslims.

Another heretical group of *zindiq*s who appeared in India are the group called ***Jamaat at-tablighiyya*** (or ***Tabligh Jamaa***). Their sect was first founded in 1926/1345 by an ignoramus named Ilyas. He asserted that Muslims had "deviated from the true path of Islam" and that he had dreamt of a "divine command" to rescue them. He was preaching what he had learned from the books by his heretical masters, namely, Nezir Husayn, Rashid Ahmad Kankuhi and Khalil Ahmad Seharanpuri. To deceive Muslims, they always talk about the importance of *salat* and *jamaa.* However, none of their *salat* or other rituals are *maqbul* (acceptable, *thawab*-deserving) since they are heretics (*ahl al-bida*), that is they are outside *Ahl as-Sunna.* The first thing they have to do is to read books written by scholars of *Ahl as-Sunna* to free themselves of heretical beliefs and become true Muslims. People who misinterpret the *ayat*s with hidden meanings in the *Quran al-Karim* are termed people of *bida* or heretics. Enemies of Islam who give such *ayat*s meanings suitable to their treacherous and heretical thoughts are called *zindiq*s, who are trying to change the *Quran al-Karim* and Islam. Such groups are founded, supported and backed financially to be spread to the whole world by the British, the greatest enemy. Members of *Tabligh Jamaa*, who are merely ignorant and ignoble tools that have fallen into the traps set by the British disbelievers, are striving to deceive Muslims by calling themselves '*Ahl as-Sunna*', by performing *salat* and by telling lies. Abdullah ibn Masud said, "There will be people performing *salat* although they believe in no religion." These people will be subjected to eternal fire at the bottom of Hell. Some of them, wearing huge turbans like stork-nests built on tops of minarets, growing beard and putting on long robes, recites and misinterprets *ayat*s to cheat Muslims. However, a *hadith sharif* states, "***Allahu Taala* judges you not by your figures and attire, but by your hearts and intentions.**"

Because these uneducated, stupid people are unable to answer the books of Hakikat Publishing, which prove their deceitful statements to be lies, they say, "Books published by Hakikat Publishing are wrong and distorted. Do not read them." The most noticeable sign to recognize heretics and *zindiq*s, who are enemies to Islam, is their saying "wrong, so shouldn't be read" about the writings of the scholars of *Ahl* *as-Sunna* and about the authentic books publishing them. The harms these people have been causing to Islam and the answers to them by the scholars of *Ahl as-Sunna* are written in detail in our book ***The Sunni Path.***]

Muhammad (*alayhis-salam*) is the highest of the prophets and is *Allahu Taala*'s compassion for all creatures. Eighteen thousand worlds of beings receive benefit from his ocean of blessings. By consensus, he is the Prophet for all human beings and genies. Many reports state that he is the Prophet for angels, plants, animals and for every substance. While other prophets had been sent to certain tribes in certain countries, *Rasulullah* (*alayhis-salam*) was and is the Prophet of all worlds of beings and all the living and lifeless creatures. *Allahu Taala* had addressed other prophets by their names. As for Muhammad (*alayhis-salam*), *Allahu Taala* favored him by addressing him, "Oh My Messenger!" The like of every miracle that had been granted to other prophets was presented to him. *Allahu Taala* bestowed upon His Beloved Prophet more gifts and granted him more miracles than those that had been granted to any other prophet. He was made superior to all the prophets with countless honors and excellences: the moon split into two when he made a sign with his blessed finger; the stones in his palm uttered the Name of Allah; trees greeted him by saying, "Oh *Rasul-Allah*"; the dry log named ***Hannana*** cried because *Rasulullah* (*alayhis-salam*) walked away and left it alone; pure water flowed from between his blessed fingers; the high grades of ***ash-Shafa'at al-Kubra*** (exclusive permission that will be given to him to intercede for ending worrisome waiting on the Day of Judgment), ***Maqaman Mahmuda*** (High Position where he, after intercession, will be thanked by Believers), ***Hawd wal-Kawthar*** (see p.77), ***al-Wasila*** (High Position of means for approaching) and ***al-Fadila*** (High Position of virtuousness) were to be given to him in the hereafter; he had the honor of seeing *Allahu Taala*'s *Jamal* before entering Paradise [during the *Miraj*]; he had the most beautiful moral quality in the world, the most perfect faith, knowledge, gentleness, patience, gratitude, ***zuhd*** (turning one's heart away from worldly things; abstention from most ***mubah***s), chastity, justness, heroism, bashfulness, bravery, modesty, wisdom, beautiful manners, helpfulness, mercy and inexhaustible honors and honorable traits. No one but *Allahu Taala* knows the number of miracles given to him. His religion abolished and invalidated all religions. His religion is the best and highest of all religions. His *umma* is higher than all other *umma*s. The *awliya* of his *umma* are more honorable than the *awliya* of other *umma*s.

Among the *awliya* of his *umma*, the one who deserved to be his successor (caliph) was **Abu Bakr as-Siddiq** (*radiy-Allahu Taala anh*), who was loved most by *awliya* and *imams* and was more suited for the caliphate than others. After the prophets, he is the highest and the most benevolent of all human beings that have come and that will come. He was the first to attain the title and honor of caliphate. As a favor and blessing from *Allahu Taala*, he had not worshipped idols before Islam commenced; he had been protected against defects such as disbelief and heresy.[1]

After him, the highest of human beings is the Second Caliph **Umar ibn al-Khattab** (*radiy-Allahu Taala anh*), whom *Allahu Taala* chose as a friend to His Beloved Prophet (*alayhis-salam*).

The next highest of human beings is the Third Caliph of *Rasulullah* (*alayhis-salam*), **Dhun-Nurain Uthman ibn Affan** (*radiy-Allahu Taala anh*), a treasure of favors and blessings and a source of modesty, faith and spiritual knowledge.

After him, the most benevolent of human beings is the Fourth Caliph of *Rasulullah* (*alayhis-salam*), **Ali ibn Abi Talib** (*radiy-Allahu Taala anh*), possessor of astonishing superiorities and the 'Lion' of *Allahu Taala*.

Next *Hadrat* **Hasan ibn Ali** (*radiy-Allahu Taala anhum*) became the Caliph (d. of being poisoned in *al-Madinat al-Munawwara* in 669/49). The thirty years of caliphate mentioned in the *Hadith ash-Sharif* was completed with him. After him, the highest human being is *Hadrat* **Husayn ibn Ali** (*radiy-Allahu Taala anhum*), the light of *Rasulullah*'s (*alayhis-salam*) eyes.

The superiority here was based on their having earned more *thawab*; abandoning their country and their beloved ones for the sake of Islam; accepting Islam before others; adapting themselves to *Rasulullah* (*alayhis-salam*) to the highest extent; following his *sunna* strictly; struggling in spreading his religion; and preventing disbelief, mischief and chaos.

Hadrat Ali (*radiy-Allahu anh*) embraced Islam before all others, with the exception of *Hadrat* Abu Bakr (*radiy-Allahu anh*), yet he was a child and had no property and lived in *Rasulullah*'s (*alayhis-salam*) house, serving him. Therefore, his embracing Islam did not cause disbelievers to be defeated, to embrace Islam or to

---

[1] It is clear by this statement about Abu Bakr as-Siddiq (*radiy-Allahu Taala anh*) how poor and ignorant people are who think and write that *Rasulullah* (*alayhis-salam*) worshipped idols before his prophetship.

follow his example. On the other hand, the other three caliphs' embracing Islam strengthened Islam. Because *Hadrat* Ali and his sons (*radiy-Allahu Taala anhum*) were *Rasulullah*'s closest relatives and of *Rasulullah*'s blessed blood, they might be said to be higher than *Hadrat* Abu Bakr and *Hadrat* Umar, but their superiority was not in every respect and did not help them surpass these great persons in every way. It was similar to Khidir's (*alayhis-salam*) having taught something to Musa (*alayhis-salam*).[1] *Hadrat* **Fatima** was higher than *Hadrat* **Khadija** and *Hadrat* **Aisha** (*radiy-Allahu Taala anhunna*) because she was closer to the Prophet in respect of blood. But one type of superiority should not show a superiority in every respect. Islamic scholars made statements disagreeing with one another on which of these three was the highest. As understood from the *Hadith ash-Sharif*, these three, *Hadrat* **Mariam** (the Virgin Mary) and the Pharaoh's wife, *Hadrat* **Asiya**, were the five highest of all the women of the world. The *Hadith ash-Sharif*, "**Fatima is superior to the women of Paradise, and Hasan and Husayn are the highest youths of Paradise**," referred to superiority only in one respect.

The next highest ones of the Companions of the Prophet (*as-Sahabat al-Kiram*) were [those six personages other than the first Four Caliphs among] ***al-Asharat al-Mubashshara***, the ten people blessed with the good news of going to Paradise. After them, the highest Muslims were the 313 Muslims who took part in the Holy Battle of *Badr*. The next were the 700 brave Muslims who took part in the Holy Battle of *Uhud*. Next to them were the ***Biat ar-Ridwan***, the 1400 Muslims who took the oath of allegiance to Rasulullah under the tree.

As-Sahabat al-Kiram (*radiy-Allahu anhum ajmain*) sacrificed their lives and property for the sake of *Rasulullah* (*sall-Allahu alayhi wa sallam*) and assisted him, so it is obligatory (*wajib*) for us to mention the name of any of them with veneration and love. It is never permissible to say words unbecoming their greatness. It is heresy to mention their names disrespectfully.

One who loves *Rasulullah* has to love all of his *Sahaba*, because a *hadith sharif* says: "**One who loves my *Sahaba* loves them**

---

[1] If blood relationship were the only criterion for superiority, *Hadrat* Abbas should have been regarded superior to *Hadrat* Ali. Moreover, Abu Talib and Abu Lahab, who were very close in respect of blood, did not even have the honor and superiority existing in the lowest Believer.

because one loves me. One who does not love them does not love me. One who hurts them hurts me. And one who hurts me hurts *Allahu Taala*. A person who hurts *Allahu Taala* will certainly suffer torture." In another *hadith sharif* he stated: "**When *Allahu Taala* wants to bless someone among my *Umma*, He places in their hearts the love of my *Sahaba*; and they love all of them dearly.**"

Therefore, the battles between the *Sahabat al-Kiram* should not be supposed to have taken place for becoming the caliph or for satisfying evil thoughts or sensual desires. It is hypocrisy which leads one to ruination to speak ill of them out of such a supposition, since jealousy and desire for position and addiction to the world had been completely cleared from their hearts by sitting in the presence of *Rasulullah* and hearing his blessed words. They were corrected and became free from greed, ambition, grudge and evil nature; they were entirely purified. Considering the fact that a person who stays for a few days in the presence of one of the *wali*s of the *Umma* of the Exalted Prophet benefits from the *wali*'s beautiful morals and excellences and becomes purified from worldly ambitions, how could it ever be presumed that the Prophet's *Sahaba*, our masters, who loved *Rasulullah* more than anybody else and sacrificed their property and lives for him and abandoned their country for him and were fond of his company, which was nourishment for spirits, were not free from bad morals, that their *nafs* was not clean and that they fought for this carrion-like temporary world? Those great people were certainly more decent than everybody. It is unfair to liken the disagreements and combats between them to matters among us, ill-willed people, or to say that they fought to satisfy their evil, sensual and worldly desires. It is not permissible to bear such improper thoughts against the *Sahabat al-Kiram*. A person who would say something against them should know that hostility towards the *Sahabat al-Kiram* means hostility towards *Rasulullah* (*sall-Allahu alayhi wa sallam*), and to speak ill of them means to speak ill of him, who educated and trained them. For this reason, the great scholars of Islam said that lack of respect for and absence of high opinion of the *Sahabat al-Kiram* meant disbelief in the Messenger of Allah. The battles of "*Jamal*" (Camel) and "*Siffin*" cannot be taken as grounds for slandering them. For the *Sahabi*s who stood against *Hadrat* Ali in those battles, there were religious reasons that protected all of them from being evil, even that caused them to be rewarded on the Day of Judgment. A *hadith sharif* says: "**One reward will be given to the *mujtahid* who is mistaken, and two or ten to the one who finds what is right. One of the two rewards is for**

employing *ijtihad*[1]. The other one is for finding the truth." The disputes and combats among those great people of Islam were not out of obstinacy or hostility but because of their [different] *ijtihad*s and out of their wish to carry out what Islam commanded. Each of the *Sahabat al-Kiram* was a *mujtahid*.[2]

It was *fard* for every *mujtahid* to act in accordance with the conclusion they found by their own *ijtihad*, even if their *ijtihad* was not in agreement with that of a *mujtahid* much higher than they. It was not permissible for them to follow another's *ijtihad*. *Al-Imam al-Azam* Abu Hanifa Numan ibn Thabit's (d. Baghdad, 767/150) two students Abu Yusuf and Muhammad ash-Shaibani, and *Imam* Muhammad ibn Idris ash-Shafii's (d. Egypt, 820/204) students Abu Sawr and Ismail al-Muzani, disagreed with their masters on many aspects, and about some of the things which their masters said '*haram*' (forbidden) they said '*halal*' (permitted), and about some of the things which their masters said '*halal*' they said '*haram*.' They cannot be said to be sinful or evil on that account. No one has said so, for they were *mujtahid*s like their masters.

It is true that *Hadrat* Ali was higher and more learned than *Hadrat* Muawiya ibn Abu Sufyan (d. Damascus, 680/60) and *Hadrat* Amr ibn al-As (d. Egypt, 663/43, *radiy-Allahu Taala anhum ajmain*). He had many superior qualities to distinguish him from them, and his *ijtihad* was more powerful and more accurate than their *ijtihad*s. However, since all the *Sahabat al-Kiram* were *mujtahid*s, it was not permissible for those two to follow the *ijtihad* of that great religious leader. It was necessary for them to act upon their own *ijtihad*s.

> **Question:** "In the battles of '*Jamal*' and '*Siffin*', a great many of the *Muhajirun* and *Ansar* among the *Sahabat al-Kiram* took part with, obeyed and followed *Hadrat* Ali. Although all of them were *mujtahid*s, they considered it was *wajib* to follow him. This shows that it was *wajib* also for *mujtahid*s to follow *Hadrat* Ali. They had to follow him even if their *ijtihad*s did not agree with his, didn't they?"

Answer: Muslims who followed *Hadrat* Ali (*radiy-Allahu Taala*

---

[1] Ijtihad: meaning, ruling or conclusion drawn by great scholars called *mujtahid*s through endeavoring to understand the hidden meaning in an *ayat karima* or a *hadith sharif*.

[2] For example, it is stated in the *Hadith ash-Sharif* in the 298th page of **Al-Hadiqa** that Amr ibn al-As (*radiy-Allahu Taala anh*) was a *mujtahid*.

anh) and fought on his side joined him not with the view of following his *ijtihad* but because their *ijtihads* were in agreement with his *ijtihad* and showed that it was *wajib* to follow *Imam* Ali. Similarly, the *ijtihads* of many prominent Companions of the Prophet did not agree with that of *Hadrat* Ali, and it became *wajib* for them to fight against him. Three different *ijtihads* of *as-Sahabat al-Kiram* came out then: some of them understood that *Hadrat* Ali was right, and it became necessary for them to follow *Hadrat* Ali; another group saw that the *ijtihad* of those who fought *Hadrat* Ali was right, and it became *wajib* for them to follow those who fought *Hadrat* Ali and to fight against him; the third group said it would be necessary not to follow either side and not to fight, and their *ijtihad* required them not to join the war. All these three groups were certainly right and deserved to be rewarded in the hereafter.

> **Question:** "The answer [above] shows that also those who fought against *Hadrat* Ali (*radiy-Allahu Taala anh*) were right. On the other hand, the scholars of *Ahl as-Sunna* have said that *Hadrat* Ali was right, that his opponents were wrong, that they were forgivable because they had an excuse (*udhr*), and that they even gained *thawab*. What can be said about that?"

Answer: *Al-Imam* ash-Shafii and Umar ibn Abd al-Aziz, two great scholars of Islam, said that it was not permissible to use the word 'wrong' about any of the *Sahabat al-Kiram*. For this reason, it was said: "It is wrong to say 'wrong' about superiors." It is not permissible for inferiors to say such words as, "He did right," "He did wrong," "We approve," or "We disapprove," about their superiors. As *Allahu Taala* did not smear our hands with the blood of these great people, so we should protect our tongues against uttering such words as 'just' and 'unjust.' Those profound scholars who studied the evidences and events and said that *Imam* Ali was right and his opponents were mistaken, in fact, meant that if *Hadrat* Ali had had the opportunity to talk with those on the other side, he would have guided them to employ *ijtihad* in conformity with his *ijtihad*. As a matter of fact, *Hadrat* Zubair ibn Awwam was against *Hadrat* Ali in the Battle of '*Jamal*' but, after studying the facts more deeply, he changed his *ijtihad* and stopped fighting. The words of the scholars of *Ahl as-Sunna* who consider the mistake as permissible should be taken as such. And it is not permissible to say that *Hadrat* Ali and those who were with him were in the right way and the other Companions of the Prophet, who were in the other group with our mother Aishat as-Siddiqa, were on the wrong way.

These combats among the *Sahabat al-Kiram* were results of

differing *ijtihads* in the branches of the *Ahkam ash-Shar'iyya* (rules of Islam). They did not have any disagreements on the essentials of Islam. Today, some people speak ill and disrespectfully of the great men of Islam such as *Hadrat* Muawiya and Amr ibn al-As (*radiy-Allahu Taala anhuma*); they cannot realize that they in effect defame and belittle *Rasulullah* (*sall-Allahu Taala alayhi wa sallam*) by defaming the *Sahabat al-Kiram*. It is written in ***Shifa ash-Sharif*** that *Imam* Malik ibn Anas said: "One who swears at and slanders Muawiya and Amr ibn al-As deserves the words one says against them. It is necessary to punish severely those who talk and write against them and who do not show respect for them." May *Allahu Taala* fill our hearts with love for His Beloved's *Sahaba*! Neither hypocrites nor sinful people but pious and Allah-fearing Muslims love those superiors.

People who realize the value and greatness of *Rasulullah*'s (*sall-Allahu Taala alayhi wa sallam*) *Sahaba* and who love and respect all of them and follow them are called ***Ahl as-Sunna***. Those who claim to love some of them and dislike others and thus slander most of them, and those who do not follow any of them, are called ***Rafidis*** or **Shiites**. There are many *Rafidis* in Iran, India and Iraq. There are none in Turkey. Some of them, in order to deceive the decent Muslim ***Alawis*** in Turkey, call themselves *Alawis*, which means 'Muslim who loves *Hadrat* Ali'. Loving someone necessitates following in their footsteps and loving those whom they love; if they loved *Hadrat* Ali (*radiy-Allahu anh*) they would follow in his footsteps. He loved all of the Prophet's *Sahaba*. He was a counselor to the second Caliph, *Hadrat* Umar, who confided his secrets to him. He married his and *Hadrat* Fatima's daughter Umm Ghulthum to *Hadrat* Umar (*radiy-Allahu anhuma*). In a *khutba*, he said about *Hadrat* Muawiya: "Our brothers parted from us, yet they are not disbelievers or sinners. Their conclusion (*ijtihad*) came out as such." When *Hadrat* Talha (*radiy-Allahu Taala anh*), who was fighting against *Hadrat* Muawiya, attained martyrdom, *Hadrat* Muawiya himself cleaned the dust from his face and became the *imam* in the funeral *salat*. *Allahu Taala* declared in the *Quran al-Karim*: "**Believers are brothers**." In the last *ayat karima* of *Surat al-Fat'h*, *Allahu Taala* declared: "**The Prophet's Companions love one another**." Not to love or, the worst of it, to bear hostility towards even one of the Prophet's Companions means disbelief in the *Quran al-Karim*. The scholars of *Ahl as-Sunna* understood the superiority of the *Sahabat al-Kiram* (*radiy-Allahu Taala anhum ajmain*) correctly and commanded Muslims to love all of them and thereby protected Muslims from catastrophy.

Those people who are called "***Kharijis***" (*Khawarij, Kharijites*) hated and bore hostility towards *Ahl al-Bait* (immediate relatives of the Prophet), that is our superiors *Hadrat* Ali (*radiy-Allahu Taala anh*) and his sons and descendants, the Sunni Muslims' dearest beloveds. Now they are called **Yazidis**. Their religion and beliefs are very heretical.

Wahhabis, while claiming to love all the *Sahabat al-Kiram*, follow not those blessed people but their own heretical way which they ascribe to the *Sahaba*. Wahhabism came about from the combination of the heretical opinions of Ibn Taimiyya, an anti-Sunni man of religious profession, with the lies of Mr. Hempher, a British spy. They do not like the scholars of *Ahl as-Sunna*, superiors of *tasawwuf* and Shiites, and they slander all of them. They suppose that they alone are Muslims. They regard people who are not like them as 'polytheists' and say that it is *halal* for them to kill and take away property of such people. Therefore, they become ***ibahis*** (or ***ibahatis***, people, for example *Wahhabis*, who say '*halal*' about killing and taking away the property of Muslims unjustly, which is *haram*). They draw wrong, heretical meanings from the *Quran al-Karim* and the *Hadith ash-Sharif* and think that Islam consists merely of those meanings. They disbelieve the *adillat ash-Shariyya* and most *hadith*s. Great scholars of the four *madhhab*s, proving with documents in many books, wrote that those who separated from *Ahl as-Sunna* went astray into heresy and caused great harm to Islam.[1]

Eyyub Sabri Pasha (*rahimah-Allahu Taala*) wrote: "Wahhabism

---

[1] For more detailed information, please read our books ***Advice for the Muslim*** and ***Endless Bliss*** in English and ***Al-minhat al-wahbiyya fir-raddil-Wahhabiyya, At-tawassuli bin-Nabi wa bis-salihin*** and ***Sabil an-najat*** in Arabic and ***Sayf ul-abrar*** in Persian. These and other valuable books written in refutation to *ahl al-bida* are published by Hakikat Publishing in Istanbul. Both in the chapter on "Baghi" in v. III of ***Radd al-muhtar*** (by Muhammad *Amin* Ibn Abidin, d. Damascus, 1836/1252) and in the chapter on "*Nikah*" in Turkish ***Ni'met-i Islam***, it is clearly written that *Wahhabis* are *ibahis*. Eyyub Sabri Pasha (d. 1890/1308), Rear-Admiral during the time of Sultan Abd al-Hamid Khan II, in his Turkish works ***Mir'at al-Haramain*** and ***Tarikh-i Wahhabiyyan***, and Ahmed Cevdet Pasha, in the seventh volume of his Turkish ***Osmanlı Tarihi (Ottoman History)***, provide detailed information about *Wahhabis*. Also Yusuf an-Nabhani, in his Arabic work ***Shawahid al-haqq*** (3rd ed. Cairo, 1965/1385), refuted *Wahhabis* and Ibn Taymiyya at length (partly reproduced within the Arabic book ***Ulama al-Muslimin wa Wahhabiyyun***, Istanbul, 1972).

appeared with a bloody, gruesome rebellion on the Arabian Peninsula in 1791/1205." Muhammad Abduh of Egypt was one of the people who tried to spread Wahhabism and *la-madhhab*ism through his books around the world. Though he was a Freemason who had openly expressed his admiration for Jamal ad-Din al-Afghani (d. 1867/1314), chief of the Cairo Masonic Lodge, Abduh was introduced to the youth as "great scholar of Islam, enlightened intellectual, eminent 'reformer'." Enemies of Islam, who were in ambush to destroy *Ahl as-Sunna* and thereby annihilate Islam, insidiously incited this mischief (*fitna*) by praising Islam in deciteful words in the disguise of people of religious position. Abduh was lauded to the skies. *Aimmat al-madhahib* (founding *imam*s of the four *madhhab*s), great scholars of *Ahl as-Sunna*, were announced to have been ignorant people. Their names were no longer mentioned. But the decent, noble descendants of our ancestors, the sons of honorable martyrs, who had sacrificed their lives for the sake of *Rasulullah* (*sall-Allahu alayhi wa sallam*) and Islam, were not deceived by these propagandas and advertisements, for which millions of pounds had been spent. They did not even listen to or acknowledge these false 'heroes of Islam.' *Allahu Taala* protected the children of martyrs against these attacks. Today, translated books of the *la-madhhabi* people like Mawdudi (founder of Al-jama'at al-Islamiyya in India, d. 1979/1399), *Sayyid* Qutb (put to death in Egypt, 1966/1386), Hamidullah and members of *Tabligh Jamaa* are being imposed upon the youth. These translations, praised exaggeratedly in gigantic advertisements, contain heretical ideas disagreeing the statements of the scholars of *Ahl as-Sunna*. We must always be on the alert and careful. May *Allahu Taala* wake up Muslims from unawareness for the grace of His Beloved Prophet Muhammad (*alayhis-salam*)! May He protect us against being deceived by the lies and slanders of the enemies! *Amin*! Let us not deceive ourselves by praying only! Praying without adhering to the *Adat al-Ilahiyya* (Divine Custom of *Allahu Taala*), without working or adhering to the means, would mean asking for miracles from *Allahu Taala*. A Muslim should both work and pray. We should first adhere to the means and then pray. The first means of escaping from disbelief is to learn and teach Islam. As a matter of fact, it is obligatory (*fard*) and everybody's primary duty, man or woman, to learn the beliefs of *Ahl as-Sunna*, ordinances and prohibitions. Today it is quite easy to learn them, because there is freedom to write and publish true Islamic books. Every Muslim must support the State which has given this freedom to Muslims.

People who do not learn the beliefs and teachings (*ilm al-hal*) of

Ahl as-Sunna and do not teach them to their children are exposed to the danger of deviating from Islam and falling into the abyss of disbelief. The prayers of such people will not be accepted. Then, how can they protect themselves against disbelief? *Rasulullah* (*sall-Allahu alayhi wa sallam*) said: "**There is Islam where there is knowledge. There is no Islam where there is no knowledge.**" As one must eat and drink in order not to die of hunger, it is necessary to learn our religion in order not to be deceived by disbelievers and not to become non-Muslims. Our ancestors frequently came together to read the books of *ilm al-hal*, learned their religion and thereby remained Muslims and enjoyed Islam. They handed this light of bliss correctly on to us. So, to remain Muslims and to avoid the risk of our children's getting deceived by the enemies inside or outside, the first and the most necessary preventive measure is to read and digest the books of *ilm al-hal* prepared by the scholars of *Ahl as-Sunna*. Parents who want their children to be Muslims should teach them how to read the *Quran al-Karim*. Let us read, learn and teach our children and those for whom we are responsible while we have the chance. It will be difficult and even impossible for them when they go to school. It will be useless to lament after the degeneration takes place. We should not believe the deceptive, false books, newspapers, magazines, television and radio programs, motion pictures and web sites of *zindiq*s and the enemies of Islam. ***Zindiqs***, as defined by Ibn Abidin (*rahimah-Allahu Taala*) in the third volume [of ***Radd al-muhtar***], are the insidious disbelievers who, although they do not believe in any religion, pretend to be Muslims and teach things that cause disbelief as if they were Islamic, and who thus strive to lead Muslims out of Islam.

Question: "A person who has read translations of the corrupt books of the *la-madhhabi* says:

" 'We should read explanations (*tafsir*) of the *Quran al-Karim*. To entrust the job of learning our religion and the *Quran al-Karim* to religious scholars is a dangerous and fearful thought. The *Quran al-Karim* does not say, 'Oh Religious Scholars!' It says, 'Oh Muslims' and 'Oh Humankind!' For this reason, every Muslim should understand the *Quran al-Karim* himself and should not expect this job from anybody else.'

"This person wants everybody to read books of *tafsir* and *hadith*. He does not recommend reading the books of *kalam*, *fiqh* and *ilm al-hal* written by Islamic scholars and superiors of *Ahl as-Sunna*. The publication of Rashid Rida's (student of Muhammad Abduh, d. 1935/1354) book ***Islamda Birlik ve Fikh Mezhebleri*** by the Turkish Chief Office of Religious Affairs (publication no. 157; in 1974/1394) caused complete confusion among readers. On many of its pages, particularly in the 'Sixth Dialogue,' Rashid Rida states:

" 'They [*muqallid*s, followers adapting themselves to one of the four *madhhab*s] elevated the *mujtahid imam*s to the degree of prophethood. Moreover, they abandoned the *Hadith* by preferring a *mujtahid*'s statement that disagreed with *a hadith* of the Prophet. They said that the *hadith* could have been cancelled (*naskh*) or there could have been another *hadith* in their *imam*'s view. By acting upon the words of those people who might have been wrong in their judging and who might have not known the matter, and by leaving aside the *Hadith* of the Prophet who was free from error, these *muqallid*s also contradict *mujtahid*s. They even contradict the Quran by doing so. They say that no one but a *mujtahid imam* could understand the Quran. Such words of *faqih*s and other *muqallid*s show that they have adopted them from Jews and Christians. On the contrary, it is easier to understand the Quran and the *Hadith* than understanding the books written by *faqih*s. People who have digested Arabic words and grammar will not have difficulty in understanding the Quran and the *Hadith*. Who on earth could disbelieve the fact that Allah is capable of explaining His own religion explicitly? Who could object to the fact that *Rasulullah* was more able than anybody else to understand what Allah meant and could explain it better than others? Saying that the Prophet's explanations were insufficient for Muslims means that he was unable to carry out his duty of propagation (*tabligh*) [of Islam] precisely. If the majority of people had not been able to understand the Quran and the *Sunna*, Allah would not have charged all people with the rules in the Book and the *Sunna*. One should know what one believes together with its evidences. Allah disapproves of *taqlid* (adapting oneself to a *madhhab*) and says that their [*muqallid*s'] imitating their fathers and grandfathers would not be deemed excusable. *Ayats* show that *taqlid* is never approved by Allah. It is easier to understand that part of the religion concerning the *furu* (Islamic rules of practices compared to beliefs) from its evidences than it is to understand the part pertaining to *iman* (*usul*; faith, beliefs). While charging with the difficult one, would not Allah charge with the easy one? It will be difficult to draw rules from some rare matters, yet then it will be deemed as an excuse not to know or practice them. Men of *fiqh* invented a number of matters (*masala*s, problems) by themselves. They produced rules for them. They attempted to introduce such things as *ra'y* (personal judgment), *qiyas jali* (obvious analogy) and *qiyas khafi* (hidden analogy) as documents for them. These things were made to overflow into the field of *ibadat* (worship, practices), on which it is impossible to acquire knowledge through reasoning. Thus they expanded the religion severalfold. They drove Muslims into trouble. I do not disbelieve *qiyas*; I say that there is no *qiyas* in the field of *ibadat. Iman* and *ibadat* were completed in the time of the Prophet. No one can add anything to them. The *mujtahid imam*s prohibited people from imitating (*taqlid*) and made *taqlid* a prohibition.'

"These statements which are selected from *la-madhhabi* Rashid Rida's book ***Islamda Birlik ve Fikh Mezhepleri***, like all *la-madhhabi* books, attemp to forbid following the *imam*s of the four *madhhab*s. It commands that everybody should learn *tafsir* and *hadith*. What would you say about it?"

Answer: If the statements written by *la-madhhabi* people are read with attention, one will easily see that they try to deceive Muslims by embellishing their heretical thoughts and separatist views with an unsound series of reasoning and false statements. The ignorant, thinking that these writings are based upon knowledge within the framework of logic and reason, may accept them, yet the learned, keen-sighted people will never be caught in their traps.

In order to warn the youth against the danger of *la-madhhabism* or anti-Sunnism, which has been driving Muslims towards eternal perdition, scholars of Islam (*rahimahum-Allahu Taala*) have written thousands of valuable books for fourteen centuries. The following is the translation of some passages from the book ***Hujjat-Allahi alal-alamin*** by Yusuf an-Nabhani (d. Beirut, 1932/1350) as an answer to the question above:

"Not everybody can draw *ahkam* (rules, conclusions) from the *Quran al-Karim*. Since even the *mujtahid imam*s would not be able to draw all the rules from the *Quran al-Karim, Rasulullah* (*sall-Allahu Taala alayhi wa sallam*) explained the rules from the *Quran al-Karim* in his *hadith*s. As the *Quran al-Karim* was explained by him only, the *Hadith* could be understood and explained by *as-Sahabat al-*

Kiram and the *mujtahid imams* only.

"In order that they could understand them, *Allahu Taala* endowed *mujtahid imams* with *aqli* (intellectual, rational and scientific) and *naqli* (transmitted, religious) knowledge, powerful comprehension, keen sight, exceedingly keen mind, and many other superior faculties. Ahead of all these virtues was *taqwa* (protecting oneself from committing *haram*). Next came the Divine Light in their hearts. With the help of these virtues, our *mujtahid imams* understood what *Allahu Taala* and *Rasulullah* meant in their words, and, as for those they could not understand, they showed [solutions for] them through ***qiyas***. Each of the four *aimmat al-madhahib* (leading scholars who founded the *madhhabs* of *Ahl as-Sunna*) informed that they did not speak out of their own opinion and said to their students: 'If you come across a genuine (*sahih*, authentic) *hadith*, leave my word aside and follow *Rasulullah*'s *hadith*!' People to whom our *aimmat al-madhahib* gave this command were profound scholars who were *mujtahids* like them. These scholars were the people of *tarjih* (a *muqallid* scholar's 'preferring', after examining, the best of the reports coming from the *imam al-madhhab* he belongs to) who knew the documents whereon the [leaders of the] four *madhhabs* based their *ijtihads*. They studied the documents and the transmitters of the *hadith* on which the *madhhab* leader had based his *ijtihad* and those of the newly encountered genuine *hadiths*, and examined which was said later and many other variables, and thereby understood which one was to be preferred. Or, the *imam al-madhhab* decided about a matter through *qiyas* because the *hadith* which would document [or solve] it did not reach him, and his students, finding that *hadith sharif*, decided differently, yet, while employing such *ijtihad*, the students did not go beyond the rules established by the *imam*. *Mujtahid muftis* who succeeded them issued *fatwa* in this manner, too. As it is understood from all that has been written here, Muslims who have been following the four *aimmat al-madhahib* and the *mujtahids* who were educated in their *madhhabs* have been following the rules of *Allahu Taala* and His Messenger. These *mujtahids* understood the rules in the *Quran al-Karim* and the *Hadith ash-Sharif*, which nobody else could understand, and conveyed what they understood. Muslims have been living up (*taqlid*) to what *mujtahids* understood and reported from the Book and the *Sunna*, because *Allahu Taala* had declared in the 43rd *ayat karima* of *Surat an-Nahl*: '**If you do not know, ask those who know**.'[1]

"Only upon the *Umma* of His Beloved Prophet (*alayhis-salam*) did *Allahu Taala* bestow the fortune that the *aimmat al-madhahib* would perform *ijtihad* and establish their *madhhab*s, and that all Muslims would come together in these *madhhab*s. *Allahu Taala*, on the one hand, created the *imam*s of *itiqad* (*iman*, beliefs) and prevented heretics, *zindiq*s, *mulhid*s and people that do Satan's work from defiling the knowledge of *itiqad* and, on the other, protected His religion from being defiled by creating the *imam*s of the *madhhab*s. Since this blessing did not exist in Christianity and Judaism, their religions were defiled and were turned into playthings.

"By consensus of the Islamic scholars, no deeply learned scholar capable of employing *ijtihad* came after the 400 years following *Rasulullah*'s (*sall-Allahu alayhi wa sallam*) death. Anyone who says that it is necessary to employ *ijtihad* in the present time must be mad or quite unlearned in Islam. When the great scholar Jalal ad-Din as-Suyuti Abd ar-Rahman (*rahimah-Allahu Taala,* d. Egypt, 1505/911) said that he had reached the grade of *ijtihad*, contemporary scholars asked him about a question to which two different

---

[1] This *ayat* shows that not everybody can understand the Book and the *Sunna* correctly and that there can be some people who cannot understand them. It commands those people who cannot understand them not to try personally to understand the *Quran al-Karim* or the *Hadith ash-Sharif* but to learn them by asking people who have understood them. If everybody had understood the meanings in the *Quran al-Karim* and the *Hadith ash-Sharif* correctly, the 72 heretical groups would not have emerged. All people who caused these groups to emerge were deeply learned, but none of them was able to understand the meanings in the *Nass* (the *Quran al-Karim* and *Hadith ash-Sharif*) correctly. Misunderstanding them, they deviated from the right way and caused millions of Muslims to end up in perdition. Some of them have been very excessive in giving wrong meanings to *ayat*s and *hadith*s, so much so that they have become as heretical as to call Muslims of the right path 'disbelievers' and 'polytheists'. In *Wahhabi*te book entitled ***Kashf ash-shubuhat***, which has been translated into Turkish and slipped into Turkey secretely, it is said that it is *mubah* (permitted) to kill and confiscate the property of Muslims who hold the belief of *Ahl as-Sunna*!

answers had been given and inquired of him to tell which answer was more dependable. He could not answer them. He said he was too busy to spare any time for it. However, what he was asked to do was employment of *ijtihad* on a *fatwa*, which was the lowest degree of *ijtihad*. Seeing that such a deeply learned scholar as as-Suyuti avoided employing *ijtihad* on a *fatwa*, what should we call those who force people to employ absolute (*mutlaq*) *ijtihad*, if we should not call them mad or ignorant of the Religion? *Al-Imam* al-Ghazali (*rahimah-Allahu Taala*, d. Tus, 1111/505) stated in his book ***Ihya Ulum ad-Din*** that there were no *mujtahids* in his time.

"If non-*mujtahid* Muslims learn a genuine *hadith* that disagrees the related ruling of the *imam* of their *madhhab* and thereupon they think that it is difficult to do it according to their *madhhab*, they have to find within the other three *madhhabs* another *mujtahid* whose *ijtihad* was based on that *hadith* and do that thing in accordance with the *madhhab* that *mujtahid* belonged to,[1] because it is not permissible for people who have not reached the grade of *ijtihad* to draw rules from the *Nass* (the *Quran al-Karim* and the *Hadith ash-Sharif*). Now some ignorant people claim that they have reached the grade of absolute *ijtihad*, that they can draw rules from the *Nass* and that they no longer need to follow one of the four *madhhabs*; they abandon the *madhhab* they have followed for years. They attempt to refute the *madhhabs* with their unsound reasoning. They make such ignorant, idiotic statements as, 'We will not follow the opinion of people of religious position who were like us.' Deluded by the Satan and provoked by their *nafs*, they claim superiority. They cannot realize that by saying so they reveal not their superiority but their idiocy and disgrace. Among them, we also see some ignorant heretics who say and write that everybody should read *tafsir* books and derive rules from *tafsir* books and from [the *Sahih* of] *Al-Bukhari*. Oh my Muslim brother! Avoid definitely making friends with such fools, supposing that they are people of religious authority and reading their fabricated books! Adhere fast to the *madhhab* of your *imam*! You are free to choose whichever you prefer of the four *madhhabs*, but it is not permissible to

---

[1] Great scholar *Al-Imam* Yahya an-Nawawi (*rahimah-Allahu Taala*, d. Damascus, 1277/676) explained this in detail in his ***Rawdat at-talibin***.

collect the facilities (*rukhsa*s) of the *madhhab*s, that is to unify the *madhhab*s, which is called '***talfiq***'.[1]

"Muslims who can read and correctly understand *hadith*s should learn the *hadith*s that were the documents of their *madhhab*, then do the actions praised and avoid those that are prohibited by these *hadith*s and, then learn the following: greatness and value of the Islamic religion; the perfect qualities of the names and attributes of *Allahu Taala* and *Rasulullah's* (*sall-Allahu alayhi wa sallam*) life, virtues and miracles; the order of this world and the next, Paradise and Hell; angels, genies, ancient *umma*s, the prophets and their heavenly books; the superior qualities peculiar to *Rasulullah* and to the *Quran al-Karim*; the lives of his *Al* (immediate relatives) and those of his *Sahaba*; the signs of the Last Day, and much more information about this world and the next. Extensive information pertaining to this world and the next has been accumulated in *Rasulullah*'s *hadith*s.

"As what is written here is understood, it becomes apparent how ignorant is the one who says that those religious decisions based by *mujtahid*s on *hadith*s are useless. Among the innumerous items of information given in *hadith*s, those *hadith*s teaching *ibadat* and *muamalat* (rules of relations between people such as commerce) are very few. According to some scholars, there are about 500 [including the repetitive ones, there are no more than 3000]; among so few *hadith*s, it is not presumable that any of the four *aimmat al-madhahib* might not have heard one genuine (*sahih*) *hadith*. Every genuine *hadith* was used as a document by at least one of the four aimmat al-madhahib. Muslims who see that a certain matter in their *madhhab* disagrees with a genuine *hadith* should perform that matter by following another *madhhab* which based its *ijtihad* on that *hadith*. Perhaps the *imam* of those Muslims' *madhhab* also had

---

[1] '***Talfiq***' means a ritual act's being compatible to none of the *madhhab*s because of its being performed by mixing the easy ways of the four *madhhab*s. After one performs an Islamic practice according to one of the four *madhhab*s, that is after one's performance is *sahih* (valid, suitable) in that *madhhab*, one's observing additionally as many as possible of the conditions that are necessary in the other three *madhhab*s with the view that the act will be *sahih* and acceptable also in these *madhhab*s is called '***taqwa***', which yields much *thawab*. In a broadest sense, *taqwa* means 'protecting oneself from committing *haram*'.

heard of the *hadith*, yet, following another *hadith* which he had understood to be more *sahih* or, being said later, cancelled the former, or, for some other reasons known to *mujtahids*, he did not take the former *hadith* as a document. For those Muslims who understands that a *hadith* is geniune, it is good to follow that *hadith* by giving up their *madhhab*'s ruling which does not conform to that *hadith*, yet, in this case they have to imitate another *madhhab* which used that *hadith* in its *ijtihad* for the matter in question, because the *imam* of that second *madhhab*, knowing those documents of that ruling unknown to these Muslims, found out that there was nothing to prevent acting upon that *hadith*. Nevertheless, it is as well permissible for these Muslims to carry out that matter in accordance with their *madhhab*, for it is doubtless that the *imam* of their *madhhab* relied upon a sound document in his ruling. Islam deems it excusable for a *muqallid* (follower of, one adhering to, a *madhhab*) not to know that document, for none of the *imams* of the four *madhhabs* deviated from the Book and the *Sunna* in *ijtihad*. Their *madhhabs* are the explanations of the Book and the *Sunna*. They explained the meanings and rules in the Book and the *Sunna* for Muslims. They explained them in a way that Muslims can understand them, and wrote them in books. This work of *aimmat al-madhahib* (*rahimahum-Allahu Taala*) was such a tremendous service to Islam that human power would not have sufficed for doing it if *Allahu Taala* had not helped them. These *madhhabs* are one of the most ideal evidences of the fact that *Rasulullah* (*sall-Allahu Taala alayhi wa sallam*) is the True Prophet and Islam is the True Religion.

"The differences in the *ijtihads* of our *aimmat al-madhahib* were only in matters pertaining to practices (*furu ad-Din*, in matters of *fiqh*). There was no disagreement among them in respect to belief (*usul ad-Din*, the knowledge of *itiqad* or *iman*). Nor did they differ from one another in those teachings of practices which are known to be essential in the Religion and which were taken from those *hadiths* whose documents were conveyed by way of *tawatur*. They differed only in some aspects of knowledge concerning practices. This arose from the difference in their understanding the soundness of the documents of these matters. This little difference among them is [*Allahu Taala*'s] grace over the *Umma*; Muslims are permitted to follow any *madhhab* they like and find easy. *Rasulullah* (*sall-Allahu Taala alayhi wa sallam*) foretold this difference as glad tidings, and it has happened as had been foretold.

"It is not permitted to employ *ijtihad* in the knowledge of *itiqad*, that is to say in the facts to be believed. It gives way to deviation and heresy. It is a grave sin. There is only one correct way in matters pertaining to belief: ***Ahl as-Sunnat wal-Jamaa***. The difference which was declared to be [*Allahu Taala*'s] grace in the *Hadith ash-Sharif* was the difference in practices.

"In a matter on which the judgments of the four *madhhabs* differ from one another, only the judgment of one of them is correct. Those who act in this correct way will be given two *thawabs*, and those who act according to one of the incorrect judgments will be given one *thawab*. Madhhabs' being [*Allahu Taala*'s] grace reveals the fact that it is permitted to leave one *madhhab* and follow the ruling of a practice in another *madhhab*, but, excepting the four known *madhhabs*, it is not permitted to follow any of *madhhabs* that belonged to *Ahl as-Sunna* nor even *as-Sahabat al-Kiram*, since their *madhhabs* were not put into written form and have been forgotten. There is now no possibility for following any *madhhab* other than the known four. *Imam* Abu Bakr Ahmad ar-Razi (*rahimah-Allahu Taala*, d. 980/370), too, reported that it had been declared unanimously by scholars of Islam that it was not permissible to follow [directly the *madhhabs* of] *as-Sahabat al-Kiram*. For those who want to understand well the superiority of the *madhhabs*, of *mujtahids*, especially of the four *aimmat al-madhahib*, the fact that their *madhhabs* did not deviate from the Book and the *Sunna* and that the rules conveyed by them through *ijma* and *qiyas* were not their own opinions but were taken from the Book and the *Sunna*, we recommend the books ***Al-mizan al-kubra*** and ***Al-mizan al-Khidriyya*** by *Imam* Abd al-Wahhab ash-Sharani (*rahimah-Allahu Taala*)."[1]

The statement, "*The Quran al-Karim* does not say 'religious scholars'," –quoted in the above question– is not correct. There are various *ayats* which praise scholars (*ulama*) and knowledge (*ilm*). *Hadrat* Abd al-Ghani an-Nablusi (d. 1731/1143) wrote in his work ***Al-Hadiqa***:

---

[1] Yusuf an-Nabhani, ***Hujjat-Allahi alal-alamin***, p. 771. The whole of the above quotation, translated from the Arabic original, contains, from other books, additions put in brackets as done in all our books, to separate them from the translated text. The Arabic original of the above passage from ***Hujjat-Allahi alal-alamin*** was reproduced by offset in Istanbul in 1974/1394.

"The seventh *ayat* of *Surat al-Anbiya*[1] orders: '**Ask the people of *dhikr* about what you do not know.**' '*Dhikr*' means 'knowledge'. This *ayat karima* commands people who do not know to find scholars and learn from them. *Allahu Taala* declared:

'**Only possessors of knowledge understand the meanings of ambiguous *ayats*'** (7, *Surat Al Imran*);

'**That *Allahu Taala* is existent and unique is understood and reported by possessors of knowledge**' (18, the same sura);

'**Possessors of knowledge said to them, "Shame on you! The rewards *Allahu Taala* will give to those who believe and do good deeds are better than worldly favors"** ' (81, *Surat al-Qasas*);

'**Possessors of knowledge and belief will say, "Well, this is the Day of Resurrection which you disbelieved** [while you were] **in the world"** ' (56, *Surat ar-Rum*);

'**Possessors of knowledge, upon hearing *al-Quran al-Karim*, will prostrate and say, "There is no defect in our Owner Who does not break His Word"** ' (108, *Surat al-Isra*);

'**Possessors of knowledge understand that *al-Quran al-Karim* is the Word of Allah**' (54, *Surat al-Hajj*);

'***Al-Quran al-Karim* has settled in the hearts of possessors of knowledge'** (50, *Surat al-Ankabut*);

'**Possessors of knowledge know that *al-Quran al-Karim* is the Word of Allah and makes** [one] **attain His approval'** (6, *Surat Saba*);

'**High ranks will be granted to possessors of knowledge in Paradise**' (11, *Surat al-Mujadala*);

'**Only possessors of knowledge fear *Allahu Taala*,**' (27, *Surat Fatir*) and

'**Most valuable among you is the one who fears *Allahu Taala* much**' (14, *Surat al-Hujurat*)."

It is declared in the *hadith*s quoted in the 365th page of the same book, ***Al-Hadika***:

"'***Allahu Taala* and angels and all creatures pray for the one who teaches people what is good**';

---

[1] The *ayats* are interpreted explanatorily, as *maal*.

‘**On the Day of Judgment, first the prophets, then the scholars and then martyrs will intercede**’;

‘**Oh Humans! Be it known that knowledge can be acquired by listening to the scholar,**’ and

‘**Learn knowledge! Learning knowledge is an *ibada.* The teacher and the learner of knowledge will be given the reward of *jihad.* Teaching knowledge is like giving alms. Learning knowledge from the scholar is like performing *tahajjud*** (*nafila*/optional ritual prayers performed at the last third of the night).’

“Tahir al-Bukhari (*rahimah-Allahu Taala*, d. 1147/542), the author of ***Khulasa,*** a book of *fatwa,* wrote: ‘Reading books of *fiqh* yields more *thawab* than performing [*nafila* ritual prayers, e.g. *tahajjud*] ritual prayers at nights, for it is *fard* to learn the *fard*s and *haram*s from [scholars or their] books. Reading books of *fiqh* in order to carry out what is learned or to teach others is better than performing *salat at-tasbih* (another *nafila* ritual prayer). It is declared in a *hadith sharif*: ‘**Learning knowledge yields more *thawab* than all extra acts of worship do, for it is useful both for oneself and for those whom one will teach**’; ‘**The person who learns in order to teach others will be rewarded like *siddiq*s** (the faithful; truth tellers).’ Islamic knowledge can be learned only from a master and from books. People who say that Islamic books and guides are unnecessary are liars or *zindiq*s, who deceive Muslims and lead them to ruination. The knowledge in religious books is derived from the *Quran al-Karim* and the *Hadith ash-Sharif.*”

Allahu Taala sent His Messenger (*alayhis-salam*) to convey, to teach the *Quran al-Karim. As-Sahabat al-Kiram* learned the knowledge in the *Quran al-Karim* from *Rasulullah.* The scholars of Islam learned it from *as-Sahabat al-Kiram*, and all Muslims learned it from the scholars of Islam and from their books. It is declared in *hadith*s: “**Knowledge is a treasure. Its key is to ask and learn**”; “**Learn and teach knowledge!**” “**Everything has a source. The source of *taqwa* is the hearts of *arif*s**,” and, “**Teaching knowledge is an atonement for sins.**”

Al-Imam ar-Rabbani (rahmat-Allahi Taala alayh) wrote in the 193rd letter of the first volume of ***Al-Maktubat:***

“A ***mukallaf*** (sane and adolescent, so religiously responsible) person first has to correct their *iman*, that is to learn the knowledge of belief written by the scholars of *Ahl* *as-Sunnat wal-Jamaa* and believe accordingly. May *Allahu Taala* plentifully reward those great scholars for their works. *Amin*! Deliverance from torture in the hereafter depends upon believing what they conveyed. Only those who follow in their footsteps will be protected against Hell. [People who follow their path are called **Sunni**.] Solely they are the ones who follow in the footsteps of *Rasulullah* (*sallallahu alayhi wa sallam*) and his *Sahaba* (*ridwanullahi alayhim ajmain*). The right and valuable teachings among the knowledge derived from the Book (the *Quran al-Karim)* and the *Sunna* (the *Hadith ash-Sharif*) are the teachings understood and reported only by these great scholars from the Book and the *Sunna*. Despite this fact, every person of *bida*, that is every 'reformer', every heretic or *la-madhhabi* person, claims that they, with their short sight, have derived their own heretical thoughts from the Book and the *Sunna*, attempting to defame and belittle the scholars of *Ahl as-Sunna*. As it is seen, not every word or writing claimed to be derived from the Book and the *Sunna* should be accepted as correct, nor should we become deceived by their gilded propaganda.

"For learning the correct belief conveyed by the scholars of *Ahl as-Sunnat wal-Jamaa*, the Persian book ***Al-Mutamad*** by great scholar *Hadrat* Tur Pushti is very valuable; it is written explicitly, so it is easy to understand.[1]

"After correction of the teachings related to belief, we should learn ***halal, haram, fard, wajib, sunna, mandub*** and ***makruh***[2] from books of *fiqh* written by the scholars of *Ahl as-Sunna* and act in accordance with them. We should not read the heretical books published by ignorant people who could not understand the superiority of these scholars. Muslims who have a belief disagreeing with the belief of *Ahl as-Sunna* will not escape going to Hell in the hereafter –may *Allahu Taala* protect us! Muslims whose belief is correct but who are slack in *ibadat* may be forgiven even if they do not repent. Even if they are not forgiven, they will be saved from Hell after torture. The main purpose is to correct one's belief. Khwaja Ubaid-Allah al-Ahrar (*qaddas-Allahu Taala sirrahul-aziz*, d. Samarkand, 1490/895) said: 'If I were given

---

[1] Fadlullah bin Hasan Tur Pushti (d. 1263/661) was a *Hanafi* scholar of *fiqh*. The book was reproduced by Hakikat Publishing in 1989/1410.

[2] These Islamic terms are used both as adjectives and nouns for the sake of simplicity in this text (see Glosssary for each).

all ***kashf***s and all ***karama***s (wonders, marvels worked by *Allahu Taala* through *awliya*) and yet if I were deprived of the belief of *Ahl as-Sunnat wal-Jamaa*, I would consider myself ruined. If I did not have any *kashf* or *karama* and had many faults, and if I were gifted with the belief of *Ahl as-Sunnat wal-Jamaa*, I would not feel sorry.'

"Today, Muslims in India are quite lonely. Enemies of Islam attack from every direction. One coin given for serving Islam today earns more reward (*thawab*) than thousands of coins given some other time. The greatest service to be done for Islam is to take and distribute books on belief and practice of *Ahl as-Sunna* to villagers and young people. Those who would be granted this service are very fortunate and happy people; they must rejoice over it and thank *Allahu Taala* very much. It is always rewarding (*thawab*-deserving) to serve Islam, yet, at such times as these when Islam is weakened through many efforts made to destroy Islam through lies and slanders, it is far more rewarding to strive to disseminate the belief of *Ahl as-Sunna*. *Rasulullah* (*sall-Allahu alayhi wa sallam*) said to his *Sahaba*: '**You live in such a time that if you obeyed nine-tenths of *Allahu Taala*'s commands and prohibitions but disobeyed one, you would perish. You would be tortured! After you, there will come such a time that people who obey only one-tenth of the commands and prohibitions will be saved.**'[1] It is the present time that the *Hadith ash-Sharif* pointed out. It is necessary to struggle[2] against disbelievers, to know who those that attack Islam are and to dislike them. For disseminating the books and speeches of the scholars of *Ahl as-Sunna*, one does not have to be a person of wonders or a scholar. Every Muslim should struggle to do it. The opportunity should not be missed. On the Day of Judgment, every Muslim will be questioned on this and will be asked why they did not serve Islam. Those who do not strive to distribute books teaching Islam and those who do not help people and institutions

---

[1] ***Mishkat-ul masabih***, vol. 1, p. 179; at-Tirmizi, ***Kitab-al Fitan***, 79th article.

[2] *Jihad* through force (*jihad qatli*) is made by the State through its army. Muslims' performing this kind of *jihad* is their undertaking as soldiers the duty given to them by the State. As also written in the 65th letter of ***Al-Maktubat***, *jihad qawli*, which is made through speech and writing, is better than *jihad qatli*.

spreading Islamic teachings will be tortured very bitterly. Excuse or pretext will not be accepted. Although the prophets (*alayhimus-salam*) were the most superior and notable of human beings, they never looked after their own comfort. In disseminating *Allahu Taala*'s religion, the way to endless bliss, they strove day and night. To those who asked for miracles they replied, '**Miracles are created by *Allahu Taala*; my duty is to report His religion.**' As they worked for this purpose, *Allahu Taala* helped them and created miracles. We, too, should disseminate the books and the teachings of the scholars of *Ahl as-Sunna* (*rahimahum-Allahu Taala*) and tell young people and our friends the evilness, baseness and deceit of disbelievers, enemies and of those who slander and persecute Muslims.[1] People who do not work for this purpose through wealth, power or profession will not escape torture. While working for this purpose, suffering distress and persecution must be deemed great happiness and a big profit. The prophets (*alayhimus-salam*), while propagating *Allahu Taala*'s commands among people, underwent the attacks of ignorant and degenerate people. They suffered very much. Muhammad (*alayhis-salam*), *Allahu Taala*'s Beloved, who was chosen to be the greatest of those great men, stated: '**No Prophet experienced so much persecution as I did.**' "

Ahl as-Sunna scholars who showed the right way to all Muslims on the earth and guided us to learn the religion of Muhammad (*alayhis-salam*) without any change or distortion were the scholars of the four *madhhabs* who reached the grade of *ijtihad*. Four of them were the most prominent. The first one was ***Al-Imam al-Azam*** **Abu Hanifa Numan ibn Thabit** (*rahimah-Allahu Taala*). He was one of the greatest Islamic scholars. He became the leader of *Ahl as-Sunna*. He was born in Kufa in 699/80 and was martyred in Baghdad in 767/150.[2]

---

[1] Telling them will not be gossip but *al-amru bil-maruf* (duty of teaching *Allahu Taala*'s commands). Every Muslim has to learn the belief of *Ahl as-Sunna* and teach it to people whom they can influence. Books, magazines and papers covering the teachings of the scholars of *Ahl as-Sunna* should be bought and sent to the youth and acquaintances. We should strive hard in order that they read them. Also, books exposing the real purposes of the enemies of Islam should be distributed.

[2] His biography is detailed in ***The Sunni Path*** and in The First Fascicle of ***Endless Bliss***.

The second one was ***Imam* Malik ibn Anas** (*rahimah-Allahu Taala*), who was a very great scholar. [In ***Radd al-muhtar*,**] Ibn Abidin wrote that he had lived 89 years in Medina from 708/90 to 795/179. His grandfather was Malik ibn Abi Amir.

The third one was ***Imam* Muhammad ibn Idris ash-Shafii** (*rahimah-Allahu Taala*), who was held in high regard by all Islamic scholars. He was born in Ghazza, Palestine, in 767/150 and died in Egypt in 820/204.

The fourth one was ***Imam* Ahmad ibn Hanbal** (*rahimah-Allahu Taala*), who was born in Baghdad in 780/164 and died there in 855/241. He was one of the 'main pillars of Islam'.

Today, people who do not follow one of these four great *imam*s are in great danger. They are in heresy. Besides them there were many other scholars of *Ahl as-Sunna* who had righteous *madhhab*s, too, but in the course of time their *madhhab*s were forgotten and could not be committed to books. For instance, the seven great Medinan scholars who were called ***al-Fuqaha as-Saba*** (the 'Seven Scholars' of *fiqh*) and **Umar ibn Abd al-Aziz, Sufyan ibn Uyayna** (d. Mecca, 813/198)**, Is'haq ibn Rahawayh, Dawud at-Tai, Amir ibn Sharahil ash-Shabi, Layth ibn Sad, Amash, Muhammad ibn Jarir at-Tabari, Sufyan ath-Thawri** (d. Basra, 778/161) and **Abd ar-Rahman Awzai** (*rahimahum-Allahu Taala*) were among them.

All the *Sahabat al-Kiram* (*radiy-Allahu Taala anhum ajmain*) were rightfully the "stars" for guidance. Any one of them would have sufficed to guide the entire world to the right way. They were *mujtahid*s, each belonging to his own *madhhab*. Most of their *madhhab*s were alike, yet, since their *madhhab*s were not collected nor written into books, it is not possible for us to follow them. The ***madhhab*s** of the four *imam*s, that is what they conveyed about the things to be believed and about the things to be done, were collected and explained by both they themselves and their students. They were committed to books. Today every Muslim must belong to the *madhhab* of one of the above-mentioned four *imam*s and live up to and perform *ibadat* (worship, rituals) in accordance with that *madhhab*.[1]

Two among the students of these four *imam*s became scholars themselves and reached very high grades in spreading the teachings

---

[1] One who does not want to follow any of these four *madhhab*s has no relation to *Ahl as-Sunna*.

of belief (*iman, itiqad*). Thus, there became two ***madhhabs* in *itiqad*** or ***madhhabs* in *iman***. The correct belief in accord with the *Quran al-Karim* and the *Hadith ash-Sharif* is only the belief shown by these two *imams*, who spread the belief of *Ahl as-Sunna*, which is the Protected Group (al-*Firqat an-najiyya*), over the whole world. One of them was **Abul-Hasan Ali al-Ashari** (*rahimah-Allahu Taala*, b. Basra, 879/226, d. Baghdad, 941/330). The other one was **Abu Mansur al-Maturidi** (*rahimah-Allahu Taala*, d. Samarkand, 944/333). In respect of belief, every Muslim has to follow one of these two great *imams*.

The paths (*turuq*, pl. of *tariq/tariqa*; 'routes', orders of *tasawwuf*) of the *awliya* (pl. of *wali*, one loved and protected by *Allahu Taala*) are right. Not to a smallest degree have they deviated from Islam.[1] *Awliya* do possess *karamat* (pl. of *karama*, wonders or marvels worked by *Allahu Taala* through *awliya*). All their *karamat* are sound and true. *Al-Imam* Abdullah al-Yafii (d. Mecca, 1367/768) said: "Ghawth ath-Thaqalayn Mawlana Abd al-Qadir al-Jilani's (*qaddas-Allahu Taala sirrahul-aziz*, d. Baghdad, 1161/561) *karamat* have been so widely known that one cannot doubt or disbelieve them since *tawatur*, that is the state of being widespread, is a *sanad* (documentary evidence for authenticity)."

It is not permissible to call, by imitating others, those people who perform *salat* "disbelievers" unless their disbelief is understood from their saying, openly and without *darura* (strong necessity or compulsion), a statement or their using something causing them to become disbelievers. We cannot curse them unless it is certainly known that they died as disbelievers. It is not permissible to curse even a disbeliever. For that matter, it is better

---

[1] In every century there have been liars and heretics who used the Religion as a means for their worldly advantages and who came forward in disguise of *walis*, *murshids* or people of religious authority. There are still evil people in every profession, in every branch of crafts and in every official position today. Seeing people who look for their advantages and pleasures in others' harm, it would be injustice or ignorance to blemish all crafts and people with whom they have had relation with; it would help religious separatists. For this reason, the existence of heretical people of religious position and ignorant, false people of *turuq* should not cause us to speak ill of Islamic scholars, people of *tasawwuf* or great personages whose honourable services have filled up annals of history. We should realize that people who slander them are unjust.

not to curse Yazid (son of and the Caliph succeeding *Hadrat* Muawiya, *radiy-Allahu anh*).

5. The fifth of the six essentials of *iman* is "**to believe in the Last Day (*al-Yawm al-Akhir*).**" It begins on the day when a person dies and continues till the end of the world. The reason it is called the "Last Day" is because there is no night to come after it, or because it comes after the world. The "Day" mentioned in this *hadith sharif* is not like the day or night we know. It denotes some time. It was not made known when the end of the world will come. No one could estimate its time. Nevertheless, our Prophet (*sall-Allahu Taala alayhi wa sallam*) pointed out many of its signs and precedents: *Hadrat al-Mahdi*[1] will come; Isa (*alayhis-salam,* Jesus) will descend to Damascus from heaven; *ad-Dajjal*[2] will appear; people called *Yajuj* and *Majuj*[3] will put the whole world into disorder; the sun will rise in the west; violent earthquakes will occur; religious knowledge will be forgotten; sinning (*fisq*) and evil will increase; irreligious, immoral, dishonest people will become leaders; *Allahu Taala*'s orders will be forbidden; *haram*s will be committed everywhere; fire will come out of Yemen; seas and mountains will split into pieces; the sun and the moon will darken; seas will mix

---

[1] *Hadrat al-Mahdi* will be a descendant of our blessed Prophet Muhammad (*alayhis-salam*). His name will be Muhammad and his father's name will be Abdullah. He will preside over Muslims, strengthen and spread Islam everywhere. He will meet Isa (*alayhis-salam*), and together they will fight and kill *ad-Dajjal.* During his time, Muslims will settle everywhere and live in comfort and ease.

[2] *Ad-Dajjal* (who is called Antichrist by Christians, and who will also be called *Masih* because his fame will spread over the world) will be a son of a Jew of Khurasan, northern Iran, and an enemy of Islam commanding innumerable soldiers. He will kill Muslims and bring discomfort and disorder to the Middle East. After shedding much blood, he will be killed by *Hadrat* al-Mahdi.

[3] It is written in the *Quran al-Karim* that *Yajuj* and *Majuj* (Gog and Magog) are two evil peoples who, at a very ancient time, were left behind a wall, and that they will spread on the earth towards the end of the world. Considering that archeological research finds cities buried under the ground and sea fossils on the peaks of mountains, that wall does not have to have been found yet, nor do those peoples have to be so numerous that we see or know them today; it can be thought that, as thousands of millions of today's people originated out of two people, those two peoples will spread on the earth multiplying out of a few people, whose place may not be known today.

with each other, boil and dry up.

A Muslim who commits sinful acts is called ***fasiq***. *Fasiq*s and all disbelievers will be tortured (*adhab*) in their graves. These facts must certainly be believed. After internment, the dead come to an unknown life and either enjoy blessings or undergo torture. As it was openly declared in the *hadith*s, two angels named ***munkar*** and ***nakir***, in the guise of two terrifying people, come to the grave to question. Questions in the grave will be on some beliefs according to some scholars or on all beliefs according to some others. For this reason, we should teach our children the answers to the following questions: Who is your *Rabb* (Owner, Creator)? What is your religion? Whose *umma* (prophet's community) do you belong to? What is [the name of] your Holy Book? Where is your *qibla* (direction turned towards during worship)? What are your *madhhab*s in *itiqad* (belief) and *amal* (deeds, *ibadat*)? It is written in ***Tadhkirat al-Qurtubi*** [by Muhammad Qurtubi Maliki, d. 1272/671][1] that those who are not Sunni will not be able to answer correctly. The graves of those who give precise answers enlarge and a window opens to Paradise. Every morning and every evening they see their [future] places in Paradise, and angels do them favors and give them good news. Those who cannot answer precisely are beaten with iron mallets so severely that every creature but humankind and genies hear them cry out. Their graves become so tight that they feel as if their bones would intertwine. Holes are opened to Hell. In the morning and in the evening they see their [future] places in Hell. They are tortured bitterly in their graves till the Resurrection.

It is necessary to believe in the Resurrection [all the dead people's becoming alive again on the Last Day]. After the flesh and bones rot and turn into earth and gas, they will come together again; the souls will enter the bodies they belong to, and all people will rise up from their graves. Therefore, this time is called the **Day of *Qiyama*** ('standing').[2]

---

[1] ***Mukhtasaru Tadhkirat al-Qurtubi*** was reproduced by Hakikat Publishing, 2000/1421.

[2] Plants absorb carbon dioxide from the air and water and salts (mineral substances) from the soil and unite them with one another and form organic substances, the living matter of our organs. It is known today that a chemical reaction taking years happens in less than a second when a catalyst is used. Similarly, *Allahu Taala* will unite water, carbon dioxide and mineral substances in graves and create organic substances and the living organs in a moment. The *Mukhbir as-sadiq* (the Truth Reporter, the Prophet) reported that we would come to the other life in this manner. And science shows that this is already being done in the world.

All living creatures will come together at the Place of Gathering (***Mahshar***) [on the Last Day]. The deed-books will fly to their owners. Almighty *Allahu Taala*, the Creator of the earth, heavens, stars and all particles, will make all these happen. His Messenger (*sall-Allahu Taala alayhi wa sallam*) reported that these would happen. It is for certain that what he said was true. All will certainly happen.

The deed-books of the pious (*salih*), good people, will be given from their right, and those of the sinful (*fasiq*), bad people, will be given from their back or left. Every action, good or evil, big or little, done secretly or openly, will be in that book. Even those deeds unknown to the *kiraman katibin* angels will be revealed by the human organs' witnessing and by *Allahu Taala*, who knows everything, and there will be questioning and settlement of accounts on every action. During the Day of Judgment, every secret action will be disclosed if *Allahu Taala* wills it so. Angels will be questioned on what they have done on the earth and in heavens, the prophets (*alayhimus-salam*) on how they announced *Allahu Taala*'s commands to people, and people on how they adapted themselves to the prophets, how they lived up to the duties revealed to them, and on how they took care of one another's rights. On the Day of Judgment, people who have *iman* and whose deeds and morals are beautiful will be rewarded and blessed, and people with a bad behavior and wrong deeds will be punished severely.

Allahu Taala, with Bounty and Mercy, will forgive all great and small sins of those Muslims whom He chooses. Except disbelief and polytheism, He will forgive every sin if He wills, and, with Justice, He will torture for even small sins if He wills. He declares that those who die in disbelief and polytheism will never be forgiven. Disbelievers with or without a heavenly book, that is people who do not believe that Muhammad (*alayhis-salam*) is the Prophet for all human beings and who disapprove even one of the rules [commands and prohibitions] he reported, will certainly be put into Hell and tortured eternally if they die as such disbelievers.

On the Day of Judgment, there will be a 'balance' (***al-Mizan***), different from those we know, for weighing deeds and conduct. It will be so large that one of its scales can hold the earth and the sky. The scale for good deeds will be bright and to the right of the *Arsh* where Paradise is, and the scale for sins will be dark and to the left of the *Arsh* where Hell is. Actions, words, thoughts and looks that are done in the world will take shapes there, and the good deeds in bright figures and the evils in dark and ugly figures will be weighed on this balance, which does not resemble worldly balances; it was said that the scale carrying the heavier load will go up and the one carrying the lighter load will go down. According to some scholars, there will be various balances, and many others said: "It was not shown clearly in Islam how and how many the balances will be, so it would be better not to think of it."

There will be a bridge called ***as-Sirat*** which will be built over Hell upon *Allahu Taala*'s command. Everybody will be ordered to cross that bridge. That day, all the prophets will entreat: "Oh Allah! Protect us!" People who are to go to Paradise will cross the bridge easily and reach Paradise. Some of them will pass with the speed of lightning, some with that of wind and some others like a galloping horse. The *Sirat* Bridge will be thinner than a hair and sharper than a sword. Adapting oneself to Islam in this world has a similar aspect; endeavoring to adapt oneself precisely to Islam is like crossing the *Sirat*. Those who endure the difficulty of struggling with their *nafs* here will cross the Sirat easily there. Those who do not follow Islam, that is who habitually follows the pleasures of the *nafs*, will cross the Sirat with difficulty. It might have been for this reason that the 'right path' shown in Islam was called the "***Sirat al-Mustaqim***" (the Straight Path) by *Allahu Taala*; this analogy shows that staying within the path of Islam is like crossing the Sirat. Those who deserve Hell will fall off the Sirat down into Hell.

There will be a body of water called ***al-Hawd wal-Kawthar*** (the 'Pool-and-River' of very delicious Nectar in Paradise) reserved for our master Muhammad Mustafa (*sall-Allahu Taala alayhi wa sallam*). It will be vast like a journey of one month. Its fluid will be whiter than milk, and its scent will be more pleasant than musk. The drinking glasses around it are more plentiful than stars. A person who drinks its fluid would never become thirsty even if they were in Hell.

It must be believed that there will be intercession (***ash-shafaa***). The prophets, *wali*s, pious Muslims, angels and those who are allowed by *Allahu Taala* will intercede for the forgiveness of small and great sins of Muslims who die without having repented, and their intercession will be accepted. [Our Prophet (*sall-Allahu Taala alayhi wa sallam*) stated: "**I will intercede for, among my *Umma*, those who commit great sins.**"] In the next world, intercession will be of five sorts:

Firstly, the sinful, becoming tired of the crowd and of waiting so long at the place of Judgment, will wail and ask that the Judgment start as soon as possible. There will be intercession for this.

Secondly, there will be intercession so that the questioning will be done easily and fast.

Thirdly, there will be intercession for the sinful Muslims so that they will not fall off the Sirat into Hell and so that they will be saved from torture in Hell.

Fourthly, there will be intercession for taking Muslims with plenty of sins out of Hell.

Fifthly, there will be intercession for the promotion of Muslims to a higher grade in Paradise where, although there will be innumerable favors and an eternal stay, there will be eight grades and every person's grade will be in proportion to the degree of their belief and deeds.

Paradise and Hell exist now. Paradise is above the seven skies. Hell is below everything. There are eight Paradises and seven Hells. Paradise is larger than the earth, the sun and the skies, and Hell is much larger than the sun.

6. The last of the six essentials of *iman* is "**the belief in *qadar*, that good (*khair*) and evil (*sharr*) are from *Allahu Taala*.**" Good and evil, advantage and harm or profit and loss coming onto human beings are all by His Will. In the dictionary, '***qadar***' means 'measuring a quantity; decision, order; muchness and largeness.' *Allahu Taala*'s Pre-eternal Will for the existence of something is called *qadar* (predestination). The [instance of] occurrence of *qadar*, that is the thing willed, is called ***qada***. *Qada* and *qadar* are also used interchangeably. Accordingly, *qada* means *Allahu Taala*'s predestination in past eternity of things that have been and will be created from eternity in the past to the everlasting future, and *qadar* means the [instance of] creation of anything just compatibly with *qada*, neither less nor more. In eternity in the past, He knew everything that would happen. This knowledge of His is called *qada* and *qadar*. Ancient Greek philosophers called it the pre-eternal favor (*al-inayat al-azaliyya*). All creatures came about from the *qada*. Also the creation of things according to His knowledge in the past eternity is called ***qada*** and ***qadar***. In believing *qadar* we should know for certain and believe that if He willed in past eternity to create something, it certainly has to exist exactly as He willed, neither less nor more; nonexistence of things He determined to create, or existence of things He determined not to create, is impossible.

All animals, plants, non-living creatures [solids, liquids, gases, stars, molecules, atoms, electrons, electromagnetic waves, every movement of every creature, physical events, chemical and nuclear reactions, relations of energy, physiological events in the living creatures,] existence or nonexistence of everything, good and evil deeds of human beings, their punishment in this world and in the next world and everything existed in *Allahu Taala*'s Knowledge in past eternity. He knew all in past eternity. Objects, peculiarities, movements and every event that happen from eternity in the past to everlasting future are created by Him in accord with what He knew in past eternity. All the good and evil deeds of human beings, their belief or disbelief in Islam, all their actions, done willingly or unwillingly, are created by *Allahu Taala*, Who alone creates and makes everything that happens through a *sabab* (cause, means, intermediary). *Allahu Taala* creates everything through some means.

For example, fire burns. In reality, *Allahu Taala* is the One Who creates burning. Fire does not have anything to do with burning. However, His Custom (*Adat*) is such that unless fire touches something He does not create burning.[1] Allahu Taala alone is the One who does the burning. He can burn without fire as well, but it is His Custom to burn with fire. If He wills not to burn, He prevents burning even in fire. He did not burn Ibrahim (Abraham, *alayhis-salam*) in fire; loving him very much, He suspended His Custom.[2]

---

[1] Fire does nothing except heating up to the ignition temperature. It is not fire that unites carbon and hydrogen with oxygen in organic substances or that supplies electron movements. Those who cannot realize the truth presume that fire does it. It is neither fire, nor oxygen, nor heat, nor the electron movement that burns or makes this reaction of burning. Only *Allahu Taala* is the One who burns it. *Allahu Taala* created all of them as means for burning. A person lacking knowledge thinks that fire burns. A boy who finishes elementary school disapproves of the words “fire burns,” and says, “The air burns,” instead. A person who finishes junior high school does not accept this and says, “The oxygen in the air burns.” A person who finishes high school says that burning is not peculiar to oxygen, but any element attracting electron burns. A university student takes into consideration energy as well as matter. It is seen that the more one knows the closer one gets to the inside of a matter and realizes that there are many causes behind the things regarded as causes. The prophets (*alayhimus-salam*), who were in the highest degree of knowledge and science and who could see the reality of everything, and the Islamic scholars, who, following in the footsteps of those great personages, attained drops from their oceans of knowledge, pointed out that each of the things supposed to be combustive or constructive today is an incapable and poor causal means and creatures, and that the Real Maker, the Real Creator, is not the means but *Allahu Taala*.

[2] As a matter of fact, *Allahu Taala* creates also substances that prevent fire's burning. Chemists have been finding those substances.

If *Allahu Taala* had willed, He could have created everything without means, burnt without fire, nourished us without our eating and made us fly without an airplane and hear from a long distance without a radio. Nevertheless, He did human beings the favor of creating everything through some intermediaries. He willed to create certain things through certain intermediaries. He hid His works under intermediaries. *Allahu Taala*'s Power was concealed behind intermediaries. He who wants *Allahu Taala* to create something adheres to its means and thus obtains it.[1]

If *Allahu Taala* did not create His Works through intermediaries, nobody would need anybody else; everybody would ask everything directly from Him and would have recourse to nothing; there would be no social relations between people such as the superior and the subordinate, foreman and workman, pupil and teacher and so forth, and thus this world and the next would be in disorder and there would be no difference between the beautiful and the loathsome, good and evil, the obedient and the disobedient.

If *Allahu Taala* had willed, He would have created His Custom in some other way, and He would have created everything according to it. For example, if He had willed, He would put disbelievers, those who are addicted to pleasures in the world, those who hurt others and the deceitful into Paradise, and He would put the faithful, worshippers and the benevolent into Hell. *Ayat*s and *hadith*s, however, show that He did not will so.

Allahu Taala is the One who creates all optional or voluntary and involuntary actions and movements of human beings.

He created option (***ikhtiyar***) and will (***irada***) in humans for His creating their optional, voluntary actions, and made this option and will a means for creating their actions. When one wants to do

---

[1] One who wants to light a lamp uses matches; one who wants to extract oil from olive uses crushing tools; one who has a headache takes an aspirin; one who wants to go to Paradise and attain infinite favors adapts himself to Islam; one who shoots himself with a pistol or who drinks poison will die; one who drinks water when in a sweat will lose one's health; one who commits sins or loses one's *iman* will go to Hell. Whatever intermediary one applies, one will obtain the thing for which that intermediary has been made a means. One who reads Islamic books learns Islam, likes it and becomes a Muslim. One who lives amongst the irreligious and listens to what they say becomes ignorant of Islam. Most of those who are ignorant of Islam become disbelievers. When one gets on a vehicle, one goes to the place it has been assigned to go.

something, *Allahu Taala* creates this action if He wills, too. If one does not want or will and if *Allahu Taala* does not will, either, He does not create. He creates upon not only one's wish; if He, too, wills, He creates, His creating one's optional actions is similar to that, when fire touches something, *Allahu Taala* creates burning of that thing, and if fire does not touch it, He does not create burning. When a knife touches something, He creates cutting. It is not the knife but *Allahu Taala* Who cuts. He has made the knife a means for cutting. In other words, He creates human optional actions for the reason (*sabab*) that the person opts, prefers and wills these actions. However, the movements in nature do not depend on human option, but are created through some other causes when only *Allahu Taala* wills. There is no creator besides *Allahu Taala*, Who alone creates substances, properties and movements of everything, of suns, particles, drops, cells, germs and atoms. However, there is a difference between the movements of lifeless substances and the optional, voluntary actions of humans and animals: when a human or an animal opts, prefers and wills an action and if He wills, too, *Allahu Taala* makes them act, and He creates their action. Humans' actions are not in humans' power. In fact, they do not even know how they act.[1] There is no option in the movements of the lifeless. *Allahu Taala* creates burning when fire touches something, and this is not a result of fire's preferring or opting to burn.[2]

Humans' optional actions happen after two factors. First, their hearts' option, will and power are involved. For that matter, their actions are called acquirement (***kasb***), which is an attribute of humans. Second, *Allahu Taala*'s creation takes place. *Allahu*

---

[1] Each action is a result of so many physical and chemical events.

[2] *Allahu Taala*, too, wishes and creates the good, useful wishes of those human servants of His whom He loves and pities. He does not wish or create the realization of their evil and harmful wishes. Always good, useful deeds are done by those beloved humans. There is many a thing which they regret having failed to do but if they thought and knew that those deeds were not created because otherwise they would have been harmful, they would not be sorry at all. Instead, they would be pleased with it and would thank Allah, who willed in past eternity that He would create humans' optional, voluntary actions after their hearts' opting and willing them; He willed it so. If He had not willed it so in past eternity, He would always create even our optional actions by force, involuntarily, without our wishing them. His creating our optional actions after we wish them is because He willed it so in past eternity. Then, the only dominant factor is His Will.

Taala's orders, prohibitions, rewards and tortures are all because *kasb* has been given to humans. In the 96th *ayat* of *Surat as-Saffat*, *Allahu Taala* says: "**Allah created you and your actions**." This *ayat* not only shows the existence of *kasb*, or the heart's option and ***iradat juziyya*** (partial free will) in the actions of humans and open proof of the nonexistence of any compulsion –for this reason, [actions are attributed to humans and] it may be said "humans' actions" just as we say, "Ali hit and broke"– but also points out that everything is created with *qada* and *qadar*.

For the creation of humans' actions, first their hearts have to opt and will it. Humans will actions which are within their power. This will or wish is called acquirement (***kasb***). Al-Amidi (*Shafii* scholar of *fiqh* and *kalam*; b. Amid = Diyar al-Bakr = Diyarbakır, 551; d. Damascus, 1234/631) said that *kasb* caused and had effect in the creation of actions. However, it would not be wrong to say that *kasb* does not have any effect in the creation of an optional action since the action wished by a human and the one created are not different from each other. Then, humans cannot do whatever they want; things which they do not want may happen, too. If humans did everything they wanted and if anything they did not wish would not happen, then they would not be humans but those who would claim divinity. *Allahu Taala*, pitying and favoring human beings, gave them power and energy only as much as they would need and as much as observance of His commands and prohibitions required. For example, one who is healthy and rich enough can perform *hajj* once in one's life; one can fast [during the days of] one month a year after the new moon for Ramadan is seen; one can perform the five-times-a-day *fard* ritual prayer (*salat*); one who has money or property equal to or more than the amount of the *nisab* can pay one-fortieth of it in gold or silver to Muslims as *zakat* one *Hijri* Lunar year after one's money or property surpasses the *nisab*. So, one does one's optional actions if one wants, and one does not if one does not want to. *Allahu Taala*'s greatness is realized here, too. Because the ignorant and fools cannot comprehend the knowledge of *qada* and *qadar*, they do not believe the statements of the scholars of *Ahl as-Sunna* and they doubt the power and option in humans. They think that humans are incapable and compelled in their optional actions. Seeing that humans cannot act optionally in some cases, they speak ill of *Ahl as-Sunna*. Such wrong statements of theirs show that they do have will and option.

Ability to do or not to do an action is a matter of ***qudra*** (power). Preferring, choosing to do or not to do an action is called ***ikhtiyar*** (option). Wishing to do what is opted is called ***irada*** (will).

Accepting a deed or not disapproving of it is called ***rida*** (consent). When power and will come together on condition that they are effective in the occurrence of something, ***Khalq*** (Creation) takes place. If they come together without being effective, it is called acquirement (***kasb***). Anyone who opts is not necessarily a creator. Similarly, everything willed is not necessarily something deserving consent. *Allahu Taala* is called *Khaliq* (Creator) and *Mukhtar* (One having Option), and the human being is called *kasib* (possessor of *kasb*) and *mukhtar* (one having option).

Allahu Taala wills and creates the ***taat***s (things and acts *Allahu Taala* likes) and sins of human beings, yet He gives consent to *taats* and dislikes sins. Everything comes into existence by His Will and Creation. In the 102nd *ayat* of *Surat al-Anam*, He declares: "**There is no god but Him (Allah), the only Creator of everything.**"

Members of the [heretical] ***Mutazila*** group, being unable to see the difference between will and consent, were confused and said: "Humans themselves create the actions they wish." They disbelieved *qada* and *qadar*. The [heretical] ***Jabriyya*** group were altogether confused; they could not understand that there might be option without creation. Thinking that there was no option in human beings, they likened them to stone and wood. They –may *Allahu Taala* protect us!– said: "Humans are not sinners. Allah is the One Who makes all evils committed." If there were not will and option in humans and if *Allahu Taala* caused evils and sins to be committed by force as the members of the *Jabriyya* said, there would not be any difference between the movements of a human who is thrown down from the mountain with fastened hands and feet and those of another human who walks down looking around. As a matter of fact, the former is compelled to roll down by force and the latter descends with their will and option. People who cannot see the difference between them are the short-sighted people who also disbelieve the *ayat*s. They consider *Allahu Taala*'s commands and prohibitions unnecessary and out of place. Presumption that humans themselves create what they wish, as the group called the *Mutazila* or *Qadariyya* (fatalism) believed, is the denial of the *ayat al-karima*, "**Allah is the Creator of everything**," as well as ascribing someone a partner, in creating, to *Allahu Taala*.

The Shiites, like the *Mutazila*, say that humans themselves create what they want. As a support they say that the donkey does not cross the rill although it is thrashed. They do not ever think that if a human wills to do something and if *Allahu Taala* does not will it to be done, these two wills cannot happen at the same time: if what

Allahu Taala wills happens, then the *Mutazila*'s argument is wrong; that is humans can neither create nor do everything they want; if whatever a human willed happened, like they say, then *Allahu Taala* would have been incapable and unsuccessful. *Allahu Taala* is far from being incapable. Only what He wills happens. He is the only One who creates everything. And such is *Allahu Taala*. It is very loathsome to say and write words like, "That person created this," "We created that," or "They created that."[1] It is rudeness towards *Allahu Taala*. It causes disbelief.

---

[1] As explained above, humans' optional actions happen through many physical, chemical and physiological events, which do not depend on their will and which they are not even conscious of. Reasonable scientists who have realized this subtlety would be ashamed to say, "We have done," let alone saying, "we have created," about their optional actions. They would feel modest towards *Allahu Taala*. A person with little knowledge, understanding and modesty, however, does not feel ashamed to say anything at any place. *Allahu Taala* has mercy upon all people on the earth. *Allahu Taala* creates whatever they need and sends them to everybody. He notifies them plainly of what they should do so that they can live in this world in peace and happiness and attain the endless bliss of the next world. He guides to the right path whomever He wishes among those who left the true way and followed the way to *kufr* (disbelief) and heresy as a result of being deceived by their own *nafs* (human desires), bad friends, harmful books, and media. He pulls them towards the right way. He does not bestow this blessing upon those who are cruel and exceed the limits. He lets them stay in the swamp of disbelief where they dropped in, liked and desired.

TWO LETTERS BY SHARAF AD-DIN MUNIRI (*rahimah-Allahu Taala*)

(THE NECESSITY OF ADHERING TO THE MEANS)

Sharaf ad-Din Ahmad ibn Yahya Muniri (d. 1380/782), one of the great Islamic scholars educated in India, wrote in the 18th letter of his Persian ***Maktubat***[1]:

> "Most people go wrong by acting upon doubts and illusions. Some of such ill-thinking people say: '*Allahu Taala* does not need our *ibada* (worship), which do Him no good. It is indifferent to His Greatness whether people worship Him or disobey Him. People who worship suffer trouble and bother themselves in vain.' This reasoning is wrong; people who do not know Islam say so because they think that *worshipping* was ordered because it was useful to *Allahu Taala*. This is a very wrong supposition and it makes one confuse the impossible with the possible. Any *ibada* done by anyone is useful to oneself only. This is declared clearly in the 18th *ayat* of *Surat Fatir* by *Allahu Taala*. One who bears this wrong thought is like an ill person whom the doctor recommends to diet but who does not diet and says, 'It does not harm the doctor if I don't diet.' One is right to say that it will not harm the doctor, but it harms one. The doctor

---

[1] There are 100 letters in this collection of ***Maktubat*** (Letters). It was compiled in 1339/741 and printed in India in 1911/1329. There is a manuscript copy in the Süleymaniyye Library in Istanbul. ***Irshad as-salikin*** and ***Madin al-maani*** are Sharaf ad-Din Ahmad ibn Yahya Muniri's (*rahimah-Allahu Taala*) two other valuable books. Yahya Muniri lived in Bihar, India, where his grave is. Munir is a village in Bihar. His detailed biography is written in Shah Abd al-Haqq ad-Dahlawi's (*rahimah-Allahu Taala*) Persian work ***Akhbar al-akhyar***, which was published in Deoband, India, in 1914/1332 and was later reproduced in Lahore, Pakistan.

recommends the patient to diet not because it is useful to the doctor but to cure the patient's disease. If one follows the doctor's advice one recovers. If one does not, one will die, and this will not harm the doctor at all.

"Some other wrong-thinking people do not perform worship at all nor stop committing prohibitions (*harams*), that is they do not practice Islam. They say, 'Allah is Gracious (*Karim*) and Merciful (Rahim): pitying humans very much with endless Forgiveness, Allah will not torture anybody.' Yes, they are right in their first statement, but wrong in their last statement. In this subject, the Devil deceives and misleads them to disobedience. A reasonable person will not be deceived by the Devil. *Allahu Taala* is not only Gracious and Merciful but also punishes very severely and very bitterly. We witness that *Allahu Taala* makes many people live in poverty and trouble in this world. He makes, without hesitation, many human creatures live in torment. Although He is very Merciful and the *Razzaq* (Continuous Sustainer), He will not give even one morsel of bread unless the trouble of agriculture and farming is undertaken. Despite being the One who keeps everybody alive, He will not let a person survive without eating and drinking, nor cure a sick person who does not take medicine. He created means for all the worldly blessings such as living, enjoying good health and owning property, and showed no mercy in depriving those who would not adhere to the means of worldly blessings. There are two kinds of medicines: material and spiritual. For curing all sorts of illnesses, giving alms and saying prayers are spiritual medicines. The *hadith*s, "**Treat sick ones among you by giving alms**!" and "**Frequent *istighfar* is the medicine for all illnesses,**" are widely known. There are quite a number of material medicines. They are learned through experiments. Use of spiritual medicine is helpful in finding material medicines as well. So is the case with attaining the blessings of the next world. *Allahu Taala* made disbelief and ignorance poisons fatal to the heart and soul, and laziness makes the soul sick; if medicine is not used, the soul becomes sick and die. The one and only medicine for disbelief and ignorance is knowledge (*marifa*). The medicine for laziness is the performance of *salat* and every *ibada*. In this world, if a person takes poison and says, 'Allah is Merciful and protects me against the harm of poison,' that person becomes ill and die. If a person with diarrhoea drinks castor oil [or if a diabetic eats sugar or starchy food], that person gets worse. Because the human body is delicate, it needs a wide variety of basic necessities [food, clothing and dwelling.] It is quite difficult to find them and prepare them so as to utilize them in conformity with Islam. To manage these works with ease and comfort, a separate force called ***nafs*** was created in humans. There was not a reason for the creation of this force in animals. Things that are necessary to the body are what the *nafs* wants to be done. It enjoys doing such things in excess. Desires of the *nafs* are called ***shahwa*** (lust). Its use of *shahwa* more than needed and without intellect's supervision gives harm to one's heart and body and to others and is a sin.[1]

"Another group of wrong-thinking people undergo *riyada* (self-denial) by suffering hunger, thus they want to rid themselves completely of their desire for entertainment and desires as lust (*shahwa*) and anger (*ghadab*), which are disliked in Islam. They think that Islam commands their removal. After suffering hunger for a long time, they see that these evil desires of theirs do not go away and conclude that Islam commands something impossible. They say: 'This command of Islam cannot be done. One cannot get rid of the habits existing in one's nature. Attempting to get rid of them is like trying to make people change their color. Trying to do something impossible is to waste one's life.' They think and act wrongly. In fact, their claim that Islam commands so is sheer ignorance and idiocy, for Islam does not command removal of the human features like wrath and lust. Such a claim is a slander against Islam. If Islam had commanded so, Muhammad (*alayhis-salam*), the master of Islam, would not have had these features. In fact, he said: '**I am a human being. Like everybody, I get angry, too**.' From time to time, he would be seen angry. His anger was always for the sake of *Allahu Taala*, Who praises the people '**who can overcome their wrath**' in the 134th *ayat* of *Surat Al Imran* of the *Quran al-Karim*. He does not praise those who do not get angry. The claim of the one who, thinking wrongly, supports

---

[1] See p.53, ***Endless Bliss,*** The First Fascicle.

removal of lust is quite groundless. The fact that *Rasulullah* (*sall-Allahu alayhi wa sallam*) married nine women (*radiy-Allahu Taala anhunna*) clearly shows that that person's statement is wrong. If one loses one's lust, they have to regain it by taking medicine. So is the case with wrath; a man can protect his wife and children with his feature of wrath, and he fights (*jihad*) against the enemies of Islam with the aid of this feature. It is owing to lust that one has children and is spoken of with honor and fame after death. These are things liked and praised by Islam.

"Islam commands not to destroy lust and wrath but to control both of them and to use them in conformity with Islam. It is similar to the necessity for a horseman or a hunter not to do away with the horse or dog but to tame it in such a manner as to utilize it. In other words, lust and wrath are like the dog of a hunter and the horse of a horseman. Without these two, the blessings of the next world cannot be hunted. However, utilizing them requires training them and using them suitably with Islam. If they, instead of being trained, become excessive and exceed the limits of Islam, they lead one to ruination. Self-denial is intended not to get rid of these two features but to tame them and make them obey Islam. This is possible for everybody. Not the use of atomic power or the discovery of things like jet planes means civilization; using them for serving humankind is civilization. And that, in turn, is attainable by following Islam.

"The fourth group of those who wrongly think deceive themselves by saying, 'Everything was predestined in pre-eternity. Before a child is born, it is determined if it is going to be ***sa'id*** (pious, deserving of Paradise) or ***shaqi*** (sinful, evil, deserving of Hell). This will not change afterwards. Therefore, it is useless to worship.' The *Sahabat al-Kiram* said the same when *Rasulullah* (*sall-Allahu alayhi wa sallam*) had stated that *qada* and *qadar* would not change and that everything had been predestined in past eternity: 'Let us rely on the eternal predestination and not perform rituals (*ibadat*).' However, *Rasulullah* replied: '**Do perform the rituals! It is easy for everybody to do what was predestined for them in past eternity**!' In other words, the one who was determined to be pious in past eternity does what the pious do in the world. This means that performance of rituals by the people who were determined in past eternity to be pious, and disobedience towards *Allahu Taala* of those who were determined in past eternity to be evil, are similar [respectively] to the behaviors of people who, being predestined to live healthfully, take food and medicine and to the behaviors of those who, being predestined to become ill and die, do not take food or medicine. People with destiny of dying of hunger or illness are unable to benefit from food or medicine. Ways of earning are opened for a person whose predestination is to become rich. The ways leading to the west are closed for a person whose destiny is to die in the east. As reported, [Archangel] Azrail (*alayhis-salam*), while visiting [the Prophet] Sulaiman (Solomon, *alayhis-salam*), looked intently at one of the people who were sitting there. The man was frightened by the angel's stern looks. When Azrail (*alayhis-salam*) was gone, he begged Sulaiman (*alayhis-salam*) to command the wind to take him to a western country so that he would escape from Azrail (*alayhis-salam*). When Azrail (*alayhis-salam*) came back, Sulaiman (*alayhis-salam*) asked why he had looked intently on the man's face. Azrail (*alayhis-salam*) said, 'I had been commanded to take away his soul in a western town in an hour. But when I saw him in your company, I could not help looking at him with astonishment. Later I went to the west to carry out the command and saw him there and took his life.'[1] As it is seen, the eternal predestination was not a command but knowledge [see p 78]. In order for the eternal predestination to take place, the man had feared Azrail (*alayhis-salam*), and Sulaiman (*alayhis-salam*) carried out his wish; the predestination in past eternity was effected through a chain of means. Similarly, one who was determined in past eternity to be pious will attain the lot of having *iman* and correcting one's bad habits by undergoing *riyada*. The 125th *ayat* of *Surat al-Anam* states: '***Allahu Taala* places Islam into the heart of His human creature whom He wishes to guide to the right way**.' People who were known in past eternity that they would become evil, that is who were predestined to go to Hell, are given the thought, 'There is no need to perform

---

[1] This event is told in detail in ***Mathnawi*** by Jalal ad-Din Rumi, who died in Konya in 1273/672.

the rituals. It was predestined in past eternity whether one would be pious or evil.' They do not perform the rituals because of this thought. Their not performing the rituals because of this thought shows that they were determined in past eternity to be evil. Similarly, one whose ignorance was predestined in past eternity is given the thought, 'Everything was predestined in past eternity. Reading or learning will be of no benefit to one if one was predestined to be ignorant,' thus they do not study or learn anything, remaining ignorant. If it was predestined for one to farm and harvest crops abundantly, one is given the lot of plowing one's field and sowing seeds. So is the case with those who were preordained as pious in past eternity to believe and perform rituals and those who were preordained as evil to disbelieve and stop rituals. Some ignoramuses, unable to understand this, say, 'What do the belief and rituals have to do with being pious from past eternity, or disbelief and stopping rituals with being evil?' With their short reason, they try to comprehend this relation and to solve everything with their own intellect. However, human reason is limited, and it is stupidity or idiocy to attempt to understand the things beyond reason's comprehension with reason. Those who think so should be judged to be fools. Isa (*alayhis-salam,* Jesus) said: 'It was not difficult for me to make congenitally blind people see, nor even to revive the dead. But I was unable to explain the truth to even one fool.' *Allahu Taala*, with Infinite Knowledge and Hidden Wisdom (*Hikma*), promotes some human creatures to the rank of angels and even to a higher grade. Some others are lowered to the grade of dogs or hogs."

Hadrat Sharaf ad-Din Ahmad ibn Yahya Muniri states in his 76th letter:

" '***Saada***' means 'piousness causing everlasting happiness, quality of deserving Paradise,' and '***shaqawa***' means 'sinfulness, state of deserving Hell.' *Saada* and *shaqawa* are like two treasuries of *Allahu Taala*. The key to the first treasury is the pious deed (*taat*, *ibada*). The key to the second treasury is sinning. *Allahu Taala* knew in past eternity whether a person would be *sa'id* (of *saada*, pious) or *shaqi* (of *shaqawa*, evil). This knowledge of *Allahu Taala* is called '***qadar***' (destiny, fate). A person who was known in past eternity to become pious obeys *Allahu Taala*. A person who was known in past eternity to become evil always commits sins. In this world, everyone can understand whether they are pious or evil by looking at their own deeds. In this way, the religious scholars who are always mindful of the next world understand whether a person is pious or evil, but people of religious post who have lost themselves in this world do not know it. Every honor or blessing comes about from obeying and worshipping *Allahu Taala* with ***ikhlas*** (sincere piousness; quality, intention or state of, doing everything only for *Allahu Taala*'s sake). Every evil or trouble originates from sinning. Trouble and misfortune come to everybody through sinning. Comfort and ease come through obedience.[1] There was a man who had spent his life praying and performing *ibada* in the *Aqsa* Mosque in Jerusalem; because he had not learned the conditions of worship and *ikhlas*, he neglected one *sajda* (prostration), so he lost so much that he was utterly destroyed. However, because the dog of *As'hab al-kahf* (the Seven Sleepers) walked for a few steps behind the *siddiq*s (the faithful, truth tellers), it, though dirty, was promoted so high that it was never lowered. This situation is very astonishing for humans; scholars have not been able to solve this problem for centuries. Human reason cannot comprehend the Divine Wisdom hidden in it. *Allahu Taala* told Adam (*alayhis-salam*) not to eat wheat but let him eat it because He knew in past eternity that he would eat it; *Allahu Taala* commanded Satan to prostrate before Adam (*alayhis-salam*) but He willed him not to prostrate; *Allahu Taala* said we should look for Him, but He did not will people without *ikhlas* to attain it. [On these matters] travelers on the Divine Way could not say anything other than that they could understand nothing. Then, how can we say anything? *Allahu Taala* does not need the belief or worship of human beings, nor would their disbelief or sinning harm Him. *Allahu Taala* never needs creatures. He has made knowledge a means for clearing away disbelief and created ignorance as a means for sinning. Belief and worship originate from knowledge, while disbelief

---

[1] This is *Allahu Taala*'s Divine Custom. No one can change this. We should not consider something that looks easy and sweet to our *nafs* as *saada*. Nor should we think of things that look difficult and bitter to the *nafs* as *shaqawa* or perdition.

and sin stem from ignorance. Good deed (*taat*) should not be omitted even if it is rather minor! Sinning should be avoided even if it may seem quite minor! Scolars of Islam stated that three things would cause three other things: good deed causes *Allahu Taala*'s *Rida* (Consent); sinning causes His Wrath (*Ghadab*); *iman* causes one to earn honor and dignity. For this reason, we should strictly avoid committing even a minor sin; *Allahu Taala*'s Wrath might be in that sin. We should regard every [Sunni] Believer as being superior to us; they may be a human being whom *Allahu Taala* loves very much. Everybody's destiny, which was determined in past eternity, can never be changed. *Allahu Taala*, if He wishes, may forgive a Muslim who has always sinned and has not done any good deed. As quoted in the 30th *ayat* of *Surat al-Bakara*, when angels asked, **'Oh** [*Allahu Taala*]! **Are You going to create the creatures who will cause chaos and shed blood over the world?'** *Allahu Taala* did not say that they would not cause chaos but said: **'I know what you do not know**.' He meant: 'I make worthy what are unworthy. I make those who are distant come near. I make those belittled honorable. You judge them by their conduct, but I look at the belief in their hearts. You take your being without sin into account; they trust themselves to My Mercy. As I like your innocence, I like to forgive Muslims' sins. You cannot know what I know. I make the Believers attain My pre-eternal blessings and fondle them all with My everlasting favor.' "

[*Al-Imam ar-Rabbani* (*rahmatullahi alayh*) wrote in various letters:

"Deeds commanded by *Allahu Taala* are called ***fards***, and those prohibited are termed ***harams.*** Those [acts, utterances, behaviors] that are neither *fard* nor *haram* and which have been declared to be permitted are termed ***mubahs***. It is called ***ibada*** (worship, rituals) to perform the *fards*, to avoid the *harams*, and to do the *mubahs* for gaining *Allahu Taala*'s consent. In order for an *ibada* to be *sahih* (correctly done, so valid; carried out with the essentials of the duty) and *maqbul* (accepted, so liked and awarded by *Allahu Taala* with *thawab)*, it is necessary (a) to learn ***ilm*** (knowledge, the essentials of performing it), (b) to practice (***amal***) compatibly with the essentials, and (c) to do it with

ikhlas, which means doing it only for attaining *Allahu Taala*'s consent and love and only because *Allahu Taala* has commanded it, without considering worldly advantages such as money, position or fame. Knowledge is obtained by reading books of *fiqh* under the supervision of a competent religious teacher, and *ikhlas* is attained by observing the words, behavior and manners of a *wali* and reading books of *tasawwuf.* Islamic knowledge consists of two components: religious knowledge and scientific knowledge. It is *fard* to learn them as much as necessary. For instance, it is *fard* to learn the form of using and dosage of a medicine one is to take, and for a person who uses an electrical implement, to acquire the necessary information on electricity. Otherwise, they may cause death.

"If Muslims, though believing *fard*s and *haram*s, do not perform *ibada* due to laziness or being influenced by bad friends and die without having repented, they will be punished in the fire of Hell until the penalties for their sins are completed. Those who do not learn what the *fard*s are or, though they know them, do not attach any importance to them and do not perform them without fear of *Allahu Taala* and without feeling sorry, will go out of Islam and become unbelievers. They will be subjected to the fire of Hell eternally. This also applies if *haram*s are committed similarly.

"If one does not learn about or does not know the essentials of a ritual, one's performance of that ritual will not be *sahih* even if one has performed it with *ikhlas.* One will be subjected to the fire of Hell as if one had not performed it at all. The ritual performed by one who knows and applies its essentials is valid and it will not cause any torture of Hell for one. However, if one has not performed it with *ikhlas*, this ritual and any of one's favors are not *maqbul.* One will not earn any reward for them. *Allahu Taala* expresses dislike for such a ritual or any of one's charitable or good deeds. An *ibada* performed without *ilm* and *ikhlas* is worthless. It will not protect one against unbelief, sinfulness and penalty. Quite a number of hypocrites who performed *ibada* likewise throughout their lifetime have been witnessed to die as unbelievers. *İbada* performed with *ilm* and *ikhlas* protects one against unbelief and sinfulness and makes one *aziz* (highly esteemed) in this world. As for one's life in the hereafter, *Allahu Taala* promises in the ninth *ayat karima* of *Surat al-Maida* and also in *Surat al-Asr* that one will be saved from torture in Hell. *Allahu Taala* is true to His promises. He certainly keeps His promises."]

ALLAH EXISTS AND IS ONE;
ALL CREATURES WERE NONEXISTENT
AND THEY WILL BECOME NONEXISTENT

We recognize the things around us through our sense-organs. Things that affect our sense-organs are called **beings** (creatures, existence). Beings' effects on our five senses are called **properties** or **attributes**, by which they are distinguished from one another. Light, sound, water, air and glass are all beings; they all exist. Beings that have size, weight and volume, in other words, that occupy a place in space are called **substances** or **matter**. Substances are distinguished from one another by their properties or qualities. Air, water, stone and glass are each a substance. Light and sound are not substances because they neither occupy space nor have weight. Every being carries **energy** or **power**; that is it can do work. Every substance can be in three states: solid, liquid and gas. Solid substances have shapes. Liquid and gaseous substances take the shape of the container they are in, and they do not have specific shapes. A substance having a shape is called an **object**. Substances are mostly objects. For instance, key, pin, tongs, shovel and nail are different objects having different shapes. But they all may be made of the same matter, that is iron. There are two kinds of substances: elements and compounds.

Changes always take place in every object. For instance, it may move and change its place or become bigger or smaller. Its color may change. It may become ill or die if it is a living being. These changes are called **events**. No change occurs in matter unless there is an exterior effect. An event that does not make any change in the essence of matter is called a **physical event.** Tearing a piece of paper is a physical event. Some power must affect a substance so that a physical event may happen to that substance. Events that change the composition or essence of substances are called **chemical events**. When a piece of paper burns and turns into ashes, a chemical event takes place. A substance has to be affected by another substance so that a chemical event may happen in that substance. When two or more substances interact and a chemical event takes place in each, it is called a **chemical reaction**.

Chemical reaction between substances, that is their affecting one another, occurs between their tiniest units called **atoms**. Every object is made of a group of atoms. Although the structures of atoms are alike, their sizes and weights are different. Therefore, we know of 118 kinds of atoms today. Even the biggest atom is so tiny that it cannot be seen through the most powerful microscope. When similar atoms come together they form an **element**. Since there are 118 kinds of atoms, there are 118 elements. Iron, sulfur, mercury, oxygen and carbon are each an element. When different atoms come together they form a **compound**. There are hundreds of thousands of compounds. Water, alcohol, salt and lime are compounds. Compounds form by the combination of two or more elements or atoms.

All objects, e.g. mountains, seas, all kinds of plants and animals are composed of 118 elements. The building stones of all living and lifeless substances are 118 elements. All substances are formed by the combination of the atoms of one or more of these 118 elements. Air, soil, water, heat, light, electricity and germs dissociate the compounds or cause substances to combine with one another. **No change happens without a cause.** In these changes, atoms, the units of elements, migrate from one substance to another or leave one substance and become free. We see objects disappear but, because we judge by their outlook, we are mistaken, for this outward "disappearing" or "appearing" is nothing but a transformation into other substances; the disappearing of an object, e.g. that of a corpse in the grave, is a change into new substances such as water, gases and earthen substances. If the new substances that come into being through a change do not affect our sense-organs, we cannot realize that they come into being. For this reason, we say that the former object disappeared, while it only underwent a change.

We see also that the nature of each of 118 elements changes and that physical and chemical events happen in each element. When an element combines with another (or others) in a compound, it ionizes, that is its atoms lose or gain electron(s), and thus the element's various physical and chemical properties change. The atom of each element is made up of a nucleus and a varying number of small particles called **electrons**. The nucleus is at the center of the atom. The nuclei of atoms of all elements except hydrogen are made up of particles called **protons** and charged with positive electricity, and **neutrons**, which carry no electric charge. The electron is a small particle that carries negative electricity and moves round the nucleus. The electrons always revolve in their orbits and change their orbits.

It is evidenced in **radioactive** elements that there are changes, called fission, taking place in the nuclei of atoms, too. Further, in these nuclear fissions one element turns into another; and some mass of matter ceases to exist and turns into energy, and this change was even formulated by the Jewish physicist Einstein (d. 1955/1375). So, like compounds, elements change and may turn from one into another. Every substance, living or lifeless, changes, that is the old one disappears and a new one comes into being. Every living being, plant or animal that exists today used to be nonexistent, and there were other living beings. And in future, none of the present living beings will remain, and some other living beings will come into existence. So is the case with all lifeless beings. All living and lifeless beings, for example the element iron and the compounds stone and bone and all particles, always change, that is the old ones disappear and others come into being. When the properties of the substance that comes into being and those of the substance that disappears are alike, one, being unable to notice this change, supposes that the substance is always existent. This is similar to a movie where a different picture comes before the eye at certain short intervals; yet, unable to notice this, the viewers suppose that the same picture moves on the screen. When a piece of paper burns and becomes ashes, we say that the paper disappeared and ashes came into being, because we notice this change. When ice melts, we say that ice disappeared and water came into being.

It is written at the beginning of the book ***Sharh al-Aqaid***:

> "Because all beings signify (*alamat*) *Allahu Taala*'s existence, all creatures are called the '***alam***' (the universe; everything other than *Allahu Taala*). Also, each class of beings of the same kind is called an *alam*, for example, the *alam* (world) of human beings, the *alam* of angels, the *alam* of animals, the *alam* of the lifeless. Or each object is called an *alam*."

It is writen in the 441st page of the book ***Sharh al-Mawaqif*** by *Sayyid* Sharif Ali Jurjani (d. Shiraz, 1413/816):

> "The *alam*, that is all beings, are creatures (***hâdith***). In other words, they had been nonexistent and they came into being later. [We also explained above that creatures always come into being from one another.] Both matter and

attributes of objects have been created later. On this subject, there have been four different beliefs:

"1) According to Muslims, Jews, Christians and fire-worshippers (*Majusis*), both matter and attributes of substances have been created later.

"2) According to Aristotle and the philosophers following him, both matter and attributes of substances were pre-eternal (*qadim*). They said that they had not come into being out of nothing and that they always existed. Modern chemistry positively proves that this argument is wrong. A person who believes so or says so goes out of Islam and becomes a disbeliever. Also, Avicenna (Ibn Sina Husayn, d. 1037/428) and Muhammad Farabi (d. Damascus, 950/339) said substances were pre-eternal.

"3) According to the philosophers preceding Aristotle, matter was pre-eternal but the attributes have been created later. Today most scientists have this wrong belief.

"4) No one has said that matter had been created later and that the attributes are pre-eternal. Greek physician and philosopher Galen (Galenus) was unable to decide on any of these four types."

Muslims prove in several ways that matter and its attributes have been created later. The first way is based on the fact that matter and all its particles are always changing. Something that changes cannot be eternal; it has to be created later, since the process of each substance's coming into being from the one that precedes it cannot go as far back as to the eternity in the past. These changes should have a beginning, that is some initial substances should have been created out of nothing. If there were not an initial substance created out of nothing, that is if the process of succeeding substance's originating from another substance preceding it went far back to endless past, there would not be a beginning for substances coming into being from one another, and no substance would exist today. The present existence of substances and their originating from one another show the fact that they have multiplied from the initial substances which were created from nothing.

Furthermore, a stone that falls from the sky cannot be said to have come from infinitude [infinite space (infinity) or time (past eternity)], since this word denotes 'having no beginning or bound.' Coming from infinitude, then, means coming from nonexistence, and something which is said to have come from infinitude should have not come at all. It would be unreasonable, non-scientific and illiterate to say, "It comes from infinitude." Similarly, humans' multiplying from one another cannot be coming from past eternity. They must have multiplied beginning with the first human who was created out of nothing. If it is claimed that there had not been a first human created out of nothing and humans' multiplying from one another had come from past eternity, no human should necessarily have existed. The case is the same with every being. It would also be unreasonable, non-scientific and illiterate to say, "So has it come and so will it go. There were no initial substances created out of nothing," regarding the substances' or beings' originating from one another. Change indicates not being pre-eternal but being created out of nothing, that is not being ***Wajib al-wujud*** (the Indispensable Existence) but being ***mumkin al-wujud*** (that may come into existence out of nonexistence and may become nonexistent while being existent).

> **Question:** "The Person (*adh-Dhat*) and Attributes of the Creator of the *alam* (all beings) are pre-eternal; does not the *alam* have to be pre-eternal, too?"

Answer: We always witness the fact that the Pre-eternal Creator changes substances and particles through various means or causes, that is He annihilates them and creates others in place of them. Whenever He wills, that is always, the Pre-eternal Creator creates substances from one another. Like creating every world of beings (*alam*), every substance and every particle through some means, *Allahu Taala* can create them without any cause or means whenever He wills.

One believing that worlds of beings are created later also believes that they will become nonexistent again. It is obvious that beings created while having been nonexistent can become nonexistent again. We see now that many beings become nonexistent.

Being a Muslim requires believing the fact that substances and objects and all beings were created from nothing, and that they will cease to exist again. We witness that objects come into existence while having been nonexistent and cease to exist again, that is their shapes and properties disappear. When objects cease to exist their substances remain, yet, as we have explained above, these substances are not eternal but were created a very long time ago by *Allahu Taala*, Who will annihilate them again on the Last Day. Today's scientific knowledge does not prevent us from believing this fact. Not believing it means disbelief in science and signifies hostility against Islam. Islam does not reject scientific knowledge. It rejects omission of learning religious knowledge and of the duties of worshipping. Scientific knowledge does not disbelieve Islam, either. In fact, it confirms and verifies it.

Because the universe came into existence later, it must have a creator who created it from nothing, since, as we have explained above, no event can take place by itself. Today, thousands of medicines, household items, industrial and commercial goods, electronic equipment and weaponry are being manufactured in factories. Most of them are produced through sophisticated calculations and after hundreds of tests. Do people say that even one of them became existent by itself? No, they say that these are made knowingly and willingly and all of them require a maker; yet, they claim that millions of things and events seen in the living and the lifeless and discovered newly and delicately throughout centuries, most of them still with unknown structures, came into being by themselves accidentally. What could this hypocrisy be if not extreme obstinacy or sheer idiocy? It is evident that there is one single Creator who makes every substance and motion existent. This creator is ***Wajib al-wujud***, that is He did not come into being after being nonexistent; the Creator must always necessarily be existent and He does not need anything for His existence. If He had not always necessarily existed, the Creator would have been ***mumkin al-wujud*** or *hâdith*, that is to say a creature as the world of beings is; like a creature, He would have been created out of nothing or, through changes, out of another creature which, too, had to be created by another creator, thus an infinite number of [successive] creators being necessary; if we think in the same way as we have explained above that changes in creatures cannot be infinite, it will be understood that there cannot be an infinite number of creators and that creation was started by a first creator, because, if creators' creating one another one after the other had gone back to past eternity, there would have been no creator to begin with, and no creator would exist. Therefore, the first non-created creator is the Unique Creator of all creatures. There is no creator before or after that Creator. The Creator, not being created, always exists. If the Creator ceased to exist for a moment, all creatures would also cease to exist. *Wajib al-wujud* does not need anything in any respect. One who has created the earth, the heavens, atoms and the living in such a regular, well-designed order should be omnipotent, omniscient, able to create at once whatever He wishes, and should be unique, but there should be no change in Him. If the Creator were not omnipotent and were not omniscient, He would not have been able to create creatures in such a regular and well-designed order. If there were more than one creator and when their wishes for creating something would not agree, the ones whose wishes were left undone would not be creators and the things created would have been all mixed up.

No change occurs in the Creator. Before creating the universe He was the same as He is now. As He created everything out of nothing, He always and still creates everything; otherwise, any change would indicate being a creature and having been created from nothing. We have explained above that He always exists and will never cease to exist. Therefore, no change occurs in Him. Just as creatures needed Him in their creation initially, so they need Him every moment. He alone creates everything and makes every change. In order for everything to be in harmony and for humans to be able to survive and be civilized, He creates everything through a means. As He creates causes, He creates their affecting and their ability to perform. Human beings act only as mediums in causes' affecting substances.

Eating when hungry, taking medicine when sick, striking a match for lighting a candle, pouring some acid on zinc for obtaining hydrogen, mixing and heating lime with clay for making cement, feeding the cow for getting milk, building a hydro-electric power-station for generating electricity and constructing any kind of factory are all examples of acting, by using the causes, as mediums in *Allahu Taala*'s creating new things. Human will and power, too, are the means created by *Allahu Taala*. Human beings are means for *Allahu Taala*'s creating. *Allahu Taala* wants to create in this manner. As it is seen, it would be an ignorant word incompatible with reason and the Religion to say, "Someone created such and such thing."

Humans have to love the unique Creator, Who creates them, makes them survive and creates and sends the things they need. They should be His servants and slaves; that is human creatures have to worship, obey and respect *Allahu Taala*. This is written at length in the letter in the "Introduction" to the current book. The Name of this Indispensable Existence, of this Unique Deity, of this God, is personally declared to be **Allah**. Humans have no right to change the Name which *Allahu Taala* personally made known. An act which would be done without having the right to do it would be a very wrong, loathsome deed.

Christians and their priests believe that there are three creators. The discussions we have presented above prove the fact that there is only one creator and that the arguments offered by Christianity and priests are spurious and heretical.

THE "*SALAFIS*"

Let me state at the very beginning that the scholars of *Ahl as-Sunna* (*rahmat-Allahi Taala alayhim ajmain*) have not mentioned anything in the name of "**Salafiyya**" or a "**Salafiyya *madhhab***" in their books. These names, fabricated later by the ***la-madhhabi*** (non-Sunni; following none of the *madhhab*s of *Ahl as-Sunna*), have spread through the books of *la-madhhabi* people translated from Arabic by ignorant people of religious duty. According to them:

> "Salafiyya is the name given to the *madhhab* which had been followed by all the Sunnis before the *madhhab*s of *Ashariyya* and *Maturidiyya* were founded. They followed in the footsteps of the *Sahaba* and the *Tabiun*. The Salafiyya *madhhab* is the *madhhab* of the *Sahaba*, the *Tabiun* and *Taba at-Tabiin*. The four great *imam*s belonged to this *madhhab*. The first book to defend the Salafiyya *madhhab* was ***Al-Fiqh al-akbar*** written by *Al-Imam al-Azam*. In his book ***Iljam al-awam anil-kalam,*** *Al-Imam* al-Ghazali reported the essentials of the Salafiyya *madhhab* to be seven. The *ilm al-kalam* (knowledge of *iman*, beliefs) of the *mutaakhkhirin* (those who came later) ensued with the emergence of *Al-Imam* al-Ghazali. Having studied the *madhhab*s of early scholars of *kalam* and the ideas of Islamic philosophers, *Al-Imam* al-Ghazali made changes in the methods of *ilm al-kalam*. He inserted philosophical thoughts into *ilm al-kalam* with a view to refuting them. Ar-Radi and al-Amidi combined *kalam* and philosophy and made them one branch of knowledge. And al-Baydawi made *kalam* and philosophy inseparable. The *ilm al-kalam* of the *mutaakhkhirin* prevented the spreading of the Salafiyya *madhhab*. Ibn Taimiyya and his follower Ibn al-Qayyim al-Jawziyya tried to revive the Salafiyya *madhhab* which later parted into two: the early *Salafi*s did not go into details about the attributes of *Allahu Taala* and about the *nass*es that were *mutashabih* (with hidden meanings). The later *Salafi*s stressed the importance of details about them. This case is clearly noticeable with the later *Salafi*s such as Ibn Taymiyya and Ibn al-Qayyim al-Jawziyya. Both the early and the later *Salafi*s are referred to as *Ahl as-Sunnat al-khassa* ('genuine' *Ahl as-Sunna*). People of *kalam* who were *Ahl as-Sunna*

made *tawil* (interpretation suitable for Islam) of some *nasses*, but the Salafiyya were opposed to it. Saying that Allah's 'face' and His 'coming' are unlike the human face and coming, the Salafiyya differs from the *Mushabbiha* (those who believe *Allahu Taala* is a material being)."

It is not right to say that the *madhhabs* of ***al-Ashari*** and ***al-Maturidi*** were founded later. These two great *imams* explained and classified the knowledge of *itiqad* (system of beliefs) that had been reported by *Salaf as-salihin* (the 'pious predecessors', Muslims of the first two centuries), and spread it in a comprehensible form for the youth. *Al-Imam* al-Ashari was in *Al-Imam* ash-Shafii's chain of followers. And *Al-Imam* al-Maturidi was a great link in *Al-Imam al-Azam* Abu Hanifa's chain of followers. Al-Ashari and al-Maturidi did not go out of their masters' common *madhhab* in *itiqad*; they did not found new *madhhabs*. These two and their masters and the *imams* of the four *madhhabs* had one single *itiqad* which is the *madhhab* in *itiqad* well known by the name ***Ahl as-Sunnat wal-Jamaa***. The *itiqad* or beliefs held by the people of this group are the same as the beliefs held by the *Sahabat al-Kiram*, the *Tabiun* and *Taba at-Tabiin*. The book ***Al-Fiqh al-akbar*** written by *Al-Imam al-Azam* Abu Hanifa defends the *madhhab* of *Ahl as-Sunna*. The word 'Salafiyya' does not exist in that book nor in *Al-Imam* al-Ghazali's ***Iljam al-awam anil-kalam***. These two books and ***Al-qawl al-fasl***[1], one of the commentaries to ***Al-Fiqh al-akbar***, teach the *madhhab* of *Ahl as-Sunna* and respond to heretical groups and philosophers.

Al-Imam al-Ghazali wrote in his book ***Iljam al-awam***: "In this book I will report that, among the groups in *itiqad*, the *madhhab* of the *Salaf* (the Predecessors) is authentic. I will explain that those who deviate from this *madhhab* become people of *bida*. The *madhhab* of the *Salaf* means the *itiqad* of the *Sahabat al-Kiram* and the *Tabiun*. The essentials of this *madhhab* are seven." As is it seen, the book ***Iljam*** mentions the seven essentials of the *madhhab* of the '*Salaf*.' Saying that they are the essentials of the 'Salafiyya' means distorting the writing of the book and misrepresenting *Al-Imam* al-Ghazali. In almost all books of *Ahl as-Sunna*, for example, in the chapter "Witnessing" of ***Ad-Durr al-mukhtar***, a very valuable book of *fiqh*, '*Salaf*' and '*Khalaf*' are defined as: " '***Salaf***' (predecessors) is a designation for the *Sahabat al-Kiram* and the *Tabiun*. They are

---

[1] The books ***Iljam*** and ***Al-Qawl al-fasl*** have been reproduced by Hakikat Publishing in Istanbul.

also called *Salaf as-salihin*. And those scholars of *Ahl as-Sunna* succeeding *Salaf as-salihin* are called ***'Khalaf'*** (successors)." *Al-Imam* al-Ghazali, *Al-Imam* ar-Radi and *Al-Imam* al-Baydawi, who was an honor to the scholars of *tafsir*, were all in the *madhhab* of *Salaf as-salihin*. Groups of *bida* that appeared in their time mixed *ilm al-kalam* with philosophy. In fact, they founded the rules of their *iman* on philosophy. The book ***Al-Milal wan-nihal*** gives detailed information on the beliefs of those heretical groups. While defending the *beliefs* of *Ahl as-Sunna* against those heretical groups and disproving their heretical ideas, these three *imam*s responded to their philosophy extensively. Their response did not mean mixing philosophy with the *madhhab* of *Ahl as-Sunna*; on the contrary, they eradicated the philosophical thoughts from the knowledge of *kalam*. There is no philosophical thought or philosophical method in al-Baydawi's work, or in the *tafsir* of Shaikh-zada, the most valuable of the former's annotations. It is a very ugly slander to say that these exalted *imam*s busied themselves with philosophy. This slander was first stated against the scholars of *Ahl as-Sunna* by Ibn Taymiyya in his book ***Al-Wasita***. Further, stating that Ibn Taymiyya and his follower Ibn al-Qayyim al-Jawziyya tried to revive the "Salafiyya *madhhab*" reflects the important difference between those who are on the right path and those who deviated into heresy. Since before these two people there was not a *madhhab* called "Salafiyya," nor even the word 'Salafiyya,' how could they be said to have tried to revive it? Before them, there was the *madhhab* of *Salaf as-salihin* which, as the one and only authentic *itiqad*, was named ***Ahl as-Sunnat wal-Jamaa***. Ibn Taymiyya tried to distort this right *madhhab* and invented many *bida*s. The only source of the books, rhetoric and heretical thoughts of present-time *la-madhhabi* people and religion 'reformers' is the *bida*s of Ibn Taymiyya. In order to convince the youth that they follow the right path, these heretics devised a horrible trick: they changed the name of "*Salaf as-salihin*" to "**Salafiyya**" so that they might introduce Ibn Taymiyya's *bida*s and heretical ideas as justifiable and drag the youth into his way. They tried to smear, with stains of philosophy and *bida*, the Islamic scholars who were the successors of *Salaf as-salihin* and blamed them for deviating from their invented name Salafiyya; they put forward Ibn Taymiyya as a *mujtahid*, as a hero that revived Salafiyya. However, the scholars of *Ahl as-Sunna* (*rahmat-Allahi Taala alayhim ajmain*), who have been the successors of *Salaf as-salihin*, have been defending *Ahl as-Sunna*'s teachings of *itiqad*, which formed the *madhhab* of *Salaf as-salihin*, in the books they have written until the present time and they inform that Ibn Taymiyya, ash-Shawkani and the like have deviated from the footsteps of *Salaf as-salihin* and have been dragging Muslims towards perdition and Hell.

People who read the books ***At-Tawassuli bin-Nabi wa bis-salihin***, ***Ulama al-Muslimin wal-mukhalifun***, ***Shifa as-siqam*** and ***Tat'hir al-fuad min danasil-itiqad,*** a preface to the latter book, will realize that the originators of the corrupt beliefs called "New Salafiyya" are leading Muslims towards perdition and demolishing Islam from within.

Nowadays some people utter the name 'Salafiyya.' Every Muslim should know very well that in Islam there is nothing in the name of the *madhhab* of Salafiyya but that there is only the *madhhab* of ***Salaf as-salihin***, who were the Muslims of the first two Islamic centuries which were praised and lauded in the *Hadith ash-Sharif.* The Islamic scholars of the third and fourth centuries are called ***Khalaf as-sadiqin***. The *itiqad* of these honorable people is called [the *madhhab* of] *Ahl as-Sunnat wal-Jamaa.* This is the *madhhab* of Islamic beliefs. The *iman* held by *Salaf as-salihin*, that is the *Sahabat al-Kiram* and the *Tabiun*, was the same. There was no difference between their beliefs. Today most Muslims on the earth are in the *madhhab* of *Ahl as-Sunna.* All the 72 heretical groups of *bida* appeared after the second century of Islam. Though founders of some of them had lived earlier, it was after the *Tabiun* that their books were written and they appeared in groups and disobeyed the *Ahl as-Sunna.*

Rasulullah (*sall-Allahu alayhi wa sallam*) was the one who established the beliefs of *Ahl as-Sunna.* The *Sahabat al-Kiram* derived these teachings of *iman* from this source. And the *Tabiun al-Izam*, in their turn, learned these teachings from the *Sahabat al-Kiram.* And their successors learned from them; thereby the teachings of *Ahl as-Sunna* reached us through *naql* (chain of transmission) and *tawatur.* These teachings cannot be explored by way of reasoning. Intellect cannot change them and will only help to understand them, that is intellect is necessary for understanding them and realizing their correctness and value. All the scholars of *hadith* held the beliefs of *Ahl as-Sunna.* The *imam*s of the four *madhhab*s related to *amal* (deeds, acts, rituals, worship; *fiqh*), too, were in this *madhhab.* Also, al-Maturidi and al-Ashari, the two *imam*s of our *madhhab* related to *itiqad* (beliefs), were in the *madhhab* of *Ahl as-Sunna.* Both these *imam*s spread this *madhhab.* They always defended this *madhhab* against heretics and materialists, who had been sunk in the bogs of ancient Greek philosophy. Although they were contemporaries, they lived at distant countries and their attackers' reasoning and behaviors were different, so the two *imams*' methods of defence and criticisms were different, which does not mean that they belonged to different *madhhabs*. Hundreds of thousands of profoundly learned scholars and *awliya* coming after these two highly-learned *imams* [over centuries] studied their books and stated in consensus that they both belonged to the *madhhab* of *Ahl as-Sunna*. The scholars of *Ahl as-Sunna* dealt with those *nasses* with explicit meanings as their direct (literal) meanings, that is they gave such *ayats* and *hadiths* their clear meanings and did not made *tawil* of such *nasses* or change these meanings unless there was a *darura* (strong necessity or compulsion) to do so. They never made any changes with their personal knowledge or opinions. People from heretical groups and the *la-madhhabi*, however, did not hesitate to change the rituals (*ibadat*) and the teachings of *iman* in accord with what they had heard from Greek philosophers and from false scientists, who were adversaries to Islam.

When the State of the Ottomans, who were guardians of Islam and the servants of Sunni scholars, broke into pieces as a result of multi-centennial endeavors of missionaries and of the disgusting policy of the British Empire with all its material forces, the *la-madhhabi* took the opportunity. With devilish lies and tricks, they began to attack *Ahl as-Sunna* and demolish Islam from within, especially in countries like Saudi Arabia, where the scholars of *Ahl as-Sunna* are not allowed to talk freely. Immeasurable gold dispensed by *Wahhabis* helped this aggression spread all over the world. According to reports from Pakistan, India and African countries, some people of religious duty with little religious knowledge and no fear of Allah were given posts and apartment houses in return for their supporting these aggressors; especially their disloyal efforts in deceiving the youth and separating them from the *madhhab* of *Ahl as-Sunna* procured them those wicked advantages.

In one of the books they wrote in order to mislead Muslim students in the *madrasas* (Islamic educational institutions) and Muslims' children, the author says: "I have written this book with a view to eliminating the bigotry of *madhhabs* and helping everybody to live peacefully in their *madhhabs*." This man means that he will eliminate the 'bigotry' of *madhhabs* by attacking *Ahl as-Sunna* and by belittling the scholars of *Ahl as-Sunna*. He thrusts at Islam with a dagger and then says he does this so that Muslims will live in peace!

At another place in the book, he says: "If one thinks [of a question] and reaches a correct conclusion, one will be rewarded tenfold. One who misses gets one reward." If this were true, everybody, whether a Christian or a polytheist, would be rewarded for their every thought and would get ten *thawab*s for their correct thoughts! See how he changes the *Hadith ash-Sharif* of our Prophet (*sall-Allahu Taala alayhi wa sallam*) and how he plays tricks! The *Hadith ash-Sharif* stated: "**If a *mujtahid* concludes correctly while he extracts rules** [related to *amal*] **from an *ayat karima* or from a *hadith sharif*, he will be given ten *thawab*s. If he is wrong he will be given one *thawab*.**" This *hadith sharif* showed that these rewards would be given not to everybody who thought but to an Islamic scholar who had progressed to the grade of *ijtihad*, and that they would be given not for their every thought but for work in extracting rules from the *nass*es [related to *amal*], for their work was an *ibada* (Islamic ritual duty). *Thawab* is given for this, too, as it is given for every *ibada*.

In the time of *Salaf as-salihin* and of the *mujtahid* scholars, who were their successors, that is until the end of the fourth century of Islam, whenever a new matter came about as a result of changing living conditions, the *mujtahid* scholars worked day and night and deduced from the four sources called *al-adillat ash-Shariyya* how the matter must be handled and all Muslims handled it by following the deduction of the *imam*(s) of their *madhhab*(s). And those great scholars who did so were given ten *thawab*s or one. After the fourth century, people went on following these *mujtahid*s' deductions. During that long period, not a single Muslim was left without solution in any of their affairs. Afterwards, no scholars or *mufti*s were educated even at the seventh level of *mujtahid*s and, therefore, today we have to learn from a Muslim who can read and understand the books of the scholars of one of the four *madhhab*s, or from the books that Muslim has translated, and adapt our *ibadat* and daily life to that Muslim. *Allahu Taala* declared the rules of everything in the *Quran al-Karim*. His exalted Prophet Muhammad (*alayhis-salam*) explained all of them. The scholars of *Ahl as-Sunna*, learning them from the *Sahabat al-Kiram*, wrote them in their books. These books exist all over the world now. The way of practicing a new thing that will come about in any part of the world till the end of the world can be solved by likening it to a piece of information in these books. This attainability is a miracle (*mujiza*) of the *Quran al-Karim* and an extraordinary marvel (*karama*) of Islamic scholars. Indeed, it is essentially important to learn how to do the affair encountered by asking a true Sunni Muslim. One who asks a *la-madhhabi* person of religious post will be misled with an answer inconsistent with the books of *fiqh*.

As reflected above, the youth are deceived by those *la-madhhabi* ignoramuses from Pakistan and India who, having stayed in Arab countries for a few years, learned to speak Arabic and wasted their time by leading a life of amusement, pleasures and sinning and attained a stamped paper from a *la-madhhabi* person that is hostile to *Ahl as-Sunna*. The youth who see their fake diplomas and hear them speak Arabic think that they are people of religious position. However, they cannot even understand a book of *fiqh*, nor do they know anything of the teachings of *fiqh* in books. In fact, they do not believe these religious teachings; they call them bigotry. In the past, the answers the scholars of Islam gave for the questions asked to them were the answers they found by looking up in the books of *fiqh*. However, the *la-madhhabi* people of religious post, being incapable of reading or understanding a book of *fiqh*, mislead the questioners by saying whatever occurs to their ignorant heads and defective minds and cause them to go to Hell. It is to this effect that our Prophet (*sall-Allahu alayhi wa sallam*) stated: "**The good scholar is the best of humankind. A bad scholar is the worst of humankind**." This *hadith sharif* shows that the scholars of *Ahl as-Sunna* are the best of humankind, and the *la-madhhabi* are the worst of humankind, because the former guide people to following *Rasulullah*, that is to Paradise, and the latter lead them to their heretical thoughts, that is to Hell.

Ustadh Ibn Khalifa Aliwi, a graduate of the Islamic University of Jami al-Azhar, wrote in his book ***Aqidat as-Salafi wal-khalaf***:

> "As Allama Abu Zuhra writes in his book ***Tarikh al-madhahibi al-Islamiyya***, some people, who dissented from the Hanbali *madhhab* in the fourth century after the Hegira, called themselves '**Salafiyyin**'. Abul-Faraj ibn al-Jawzi (*rahmat-Allahi Taala alayh*), also a Hanbali, and other scholars, by proclaiming that those "*Salafis*" were not the followers of *Salaf as-salihin* and that they were holders of *bida* belonging to the cult of Mujassima, prevented this *fitna* from spreading. In the seventh century Ibn Taymiyya incited this *fitna* again."[1]

---

[1] ***Aqidat as-Salafi wal-khalaf***, 340 pages, printed in Damascus in 1978/1398; several heresies (*bidas*) of the "*Salafis*" and *Wahhabis*, their slanders about *Ahl as-Sunna* and the replies to them are written in detail.

The *la-madhhabi* have adopted the name 'Salafiyya' and call Ibn Taymiyya the "great *imam* (leader) of the *Salafi*s." This is true in one respect since the term '*Salafi*' had not existed before him. There had existed *Salaf as-salihin* whose *madhhab* was *Ahl as-Sunna.* Ibn Taymiyya's heretical beliefs became a source for *Wahhabis* and other *la-madhhabi* people. Ibn Taymiyya had been educated in the *Hanbali madhhab*, that is he had been a Sunni. However, as he increased his knowledge and reached the grade of *fatwa*, he began to admire his own opinions and assumed superiority to the scholars of *Ahl as-Sunna* (*rahmat-Allahi Taala alayhim ajmain*). Increase in his knowledge brought about his heresy. He was no longer in the *Hanbali madhhab* because being in one of the four *madhhab*s required holding the beliefs of *Ahl as-Sunna.* A person who does not have the beliefs of *Ahl as-Sunna* cannot be said to be in the *Hanbali madhhab.*

The *la-madhhabi* take every opportunity to speak ill of the Sunni Muslims of religious duty in their own country. They play all kinds of tricks to prevent Sunni books from being read and the teachings of *Ahl as-Sunna* from being learned. For example, a *la-madhhabi* person, mentioning my name said, "What's a pharmacist's or a chemical engineer's business in religious knowledge? He must work in his own branch and not meddle with our business." What an ignorant and idiotic assertion! He thinks that a scientist will not have religious knowledge. He is unaware of the fact that Muslim scientists observe the Divine Power (*Sun' al-Ilahi*) every moment, realize the Supreme Creator's Perfections that are exhibited in what has been written about Creation and, seeing the creatures' incapability compared with *Allahu Taala*'s Infinite Power, continuously gorify (*tasbih*) *Allahu Taala* and perceive that He is far from all defects (*tanzih*). Max Planck, a famous German nuclear physicist, expressed this very plainly in his work ***Der Strom.*** This *la-madhhabi* ignoramus, however, relying on a paper he might have obtained from a foreign heretic like himself and on the chair provided by heretics, and perhaps enraptured with the fancy of the gold distributed from abroad, presumes that he has monopoly on religious knowledge. May *Allahu Taala* guide this wretched person and all of us. May He also protect the innocent youth from the traps of such thieves of religion who use false documentation. *Amin*!

In fact, I humbly served my nation for more than 30 years as a pharmacist and chemical engineer. Besides, acquiring religious education and working day and night for seven years, I was honored with the *ijaza* (diploma testifying to the holder's authority on Islamic knowledge) given by a great Islamic scholar. Crushed under the greatness of scientific and religious knowledge, I fully saw my incapability. In this understanding I tried to be a deserving servant of *Allahu Taala.* The greatest of my fears and worries was to presume, by falling for the charms of my diplomas and *ijaza*, that I was an authority on these subjects. High level of my fear can clearly be seen in all my words. I never attempted to write my own ideas or opinions in any of my books. I always presented my young brothers the valuable writings of the scholars of *Ahl as-Sunna* that were admired by those who understood their value by translating them from Arabic or Persian. My fear being great, I had had no thought of writing a book; I began to ponder when I saw the *Hadith ash-Sharif* on the first page of ***As-Sawaiq al-muhriqa***: "**When *fitna* becomes widespread, one who knows the truth must inform others. Should they not do so, may they be accursed by Allah and by all people!**" On the one hand, as I learned of the superiority of the Sunni scholars' understanding and mental capacity in religious knowledge and in the scientific knowledge of their time and their efforts in *ibadat* and *taqwa*, I was humbled and deemed my own knowledge a mere drop compared to the ocean of knowledge of those great scholars. On the other hand, seeing that fewer and fewer pious people could read and understand the books written by the scholars of *Ahl as-Sunna* and that ignorant heretics had joined themselves with people of religious duty and had written heretical and heretical books, I felt grieved; the threat of damnation declared in the *Hadith ash-Sharif* frightened me. Also the mercy and compassion I felt for my dear young brothers compelling me to serve them, I began to translate my selections from the books of the scholars of *Ahl as-Sunna.* Alongside the innumerable letters of congratulation and appreciation that I have received, now and then I came across criticism and vilification from *la-madhhabi* people. Because I had no doubt in my conscience about my own *ikhlas* and loyalty to my Creator, I carried on with my service trusting myself to *Allahu Taala* and seeking *tawassul* (intercession) of the blessed souls of His Messenger (*sall-Allahu Taala alayhi wa sallam*) and of His devoted servants. May *Allahu Taala* keep all of us on the True Way He is pleased with! *Amin.*

The great Hanafi scholar Muhammad Bahit al-Mutii, a professor at Jami al-Azhar University in Egypt, wrote in his book

***Tat'hir al-fuad min danisil-itiqad*:**

"Among all human beings, the prophets (*alayhimus-salatu was-salam*) had the highest and most mature souls. They were protected from being wrong, erring, unawareness, disloyalty, bigotry, obstinacy, following the *nafs*, grudge and hatred. The prophets reported and explained what had been revealed to them by *Allahu Taala*. The religious teachings, commands and prohibitions reported by them are all true. None are wrong or corrupt. After them, the highest and most mature people were their companions (*sahaba*) since they were trained, matured and purified in the *suhba* (companionship of a prophet or a *wali*) of the prophets. They always conveyed and explained what they had heard from the prophets. All of what they conveyed, too, are true, and they are far from the aforesaid vices. They did not contradict one another out of bigotry or obstinacy, nor did they follow their *nafs*. The *Sahabat al-Kiram*'s explaining the *ayat*s and *hadith*s and employing *ijtihad* for propagating *Allahu Taala*'s religion among His human servants were His great blessing upon the *umma* of His beloved Prophet, Muhammad (*alayhis-salam*) and His compassion for him. The *Quran al-Karim* declares that the *Sahabat al-Kiram* were stern towards disbelievers but tender and endearing with one another, that they performed *salat* diligently, and that they expected everything and Paradise from *Allahu Taala*. Among their *ijtihad*s, all those on which consensus (*ijma*) was reached were right. They all deserved to attain *thawab* since the truth was only one.

"The highest people after the *Sahabat al-Kiram* were the Muslims who saw them and were trained in their *suhba*. They are called the *Tabiun*. They acquired all their religious knowledge from the *Sahabat al-Kiram*. The highest people next to the *Tabiun* were the Muslims who saw the *Tabiun* and were trained in their *suhba*. They are called *Taba at-Tabiin*. Among the people coming in the centuries after them until the end of the world, the highest and the best ones are those who adapt themselves to them, learn their teachings and follow in their footsteps. Among people of religious occupation coming after *Salaf as-salihin*, intelligent, wise ones whose words and deeds have agreed with the teachings of *Rasulullah* and *Salaf as-salihin*, and who have never diverged from their way in beliefs and deeds, and who have not exceeded the limits of Islam, have not feared others' speaking ill of them. By following them, they have not separated from the right path. They have not listened to the words of the ignorant. By following their intellects, they have not gone out of the four *madhhab*s of the *mujtahid imam*s. Muslims must find such scholars, ask them and learn what they do not know and should follow their advices in everything they do, because such scholars know and let people know the spiritual medicines, that is knowledge of curing the soul, which *Allahu Taala* created to protect His human servants from erring and to make them always act correctly; they can cure those whose souls are sick and whose comprehension is limited. Whatever such scholars say, do or believe is conformable to Islam. They understand everything correctly and answer every question correctly. *Allahu Taala* is *radi* (giving consent to, pleased, satisfied) with everything they do. To those who want to attain His *rida* (approval), *Allahu Taala* shows the ways of attaining His *rida*. *Allahu Taala* saves those who have *iman* and who fulfill the requirements of *iman* from oppression and trouble. He makes them attain spiritual radiance (*nur*), peace and happiness. Always, and in everything they do, they are in ease and comfort. On the Day of Resurrection, they will be beside the prophets, the *siddiq*s (those faithfully loyal to the Prophet; the good, always telling the truth), martyrs and *salih* (pious, avoiding sins) Muslims.

"No matter in what century they live, if those people of religious positions do not follow the statements of the Prophet and the *Sahaba*, if their words, deeds and beliefs do not agree with their teachings, if they follow their *nafs* and own thoughts and exceed the limits of Islam, or if they, following their own intellect, oppose the delicate aspects of Islam and overstep the boundaries of the four *madhhab*s in those teachings which they cannot understand, they will be judged to be corrupt people of religious positions. *Allahu Taala* has sealed their hearts; their eyes cannot see the right way, and their ears cannot hear the right word. There will be bitter torture for them in the hereafter. *Allahu Taala* does not like them. People of this sort are the prophets' opponents. They think that they are in the right way. They like their own behavior. However, they are Satan's followers. Very few of them come to their senses and resume the right way. Everything they say seems polite, delightful or useful, but all of what they think and like are evil. They deceive idiots and lead them to heresy and perdition. Their words look bright and spotless like snow, but, exposed to the sun of truth, they melt away. These evil people of religious positions, whose hearts have been blackened and sealed by *Allahu Taala*, are called ***ahl al-bida*** or *la-madhhabi* people of religious occupation. They are people whose beliefs and deeds are not compatible with the *Quran al-Karim*, with the *Hadith ash-Sharif* or with *ijma* al-*Umma*. Having diverged from the right way themselves, they mislead Muslims into perdition, too. People who follow them will end up in Hell. There were many such heretics in the time of *Salaf as-salihin* and among the people of religious position that came after them. Their presence among Muslims is like gangrene [or cancer] at a part of the body. Unless this part is done away with, the healthy parts will not escape the disaster. They are like people affected with a contagious disease. People who have contact with them will suffer harm. We must keep away from them to avoid the risk of suffering harm from them."

One of the corrupt, heretical people of religious position who have been very harmful was Ibn Taymiyya. In his books, particularly in ***Al-Wasita***, he disagreed with ***ijma al-Muslimin***, contradicted the clear declarations in the *Quran al-Karim* and the *Hadith ash-Sharif* and did not follow the way of *Salaf as-salihin*. Following his defective mind and corrupt thoughts, he deviated into heresy. He was a man of extensive knowledge. *Allahu Taala* made his knowledge the cause of his heresy and perdition. He followed the desires of his *nafs*. He tried to spread his wrong and heretical ideas in the name of truth.

The great scholar Ibn Hajar al-Makki (rahmat-Allahi Taala alayh) wrote in his book ***Al-Fatawa al-hadithiyya***:

"*Allahu Taala* made Ibn Taymiyya tumble into heresy and perdition. He made him 'blind' and 'deaf'. Many scholars informed and proved with documents that his deeds were corrupt and his statements were false. People who read the books of the great Islamic scholars Abul

Hasan as-Subki, his son Taj ad-Din as-Subki, *Imam* al-Izz ibn Jamaa and those who study the statements said and written in response to him by the Shafii, Maliki and Hanafi scholars living in his time will see well that we are right.

"Ibn Taymiyya spoke ill of and slandered the scholars of *tasawwuf.* Furthermore, he did not hesitate to attack *Hadrat* Umar and *Hadrat* Ali, who were the chief pillars of Islam. His words exceeded the proper limit and decency, and he threw arrows even at 'steep cliffs' [monumental personages]. He described the scholars of the right way as holders of *bida*, heretics and ignoramuses.

"He said, 'Corrupt ideas of Greek philosophers disagreeing with Islam were placed in the books of superiors of *tasawwuf*,' and attempted to prove it with his wrong, heretical thoughts. Young Muslims who do not know the truth may be misled by his ardent, deceitful writings. For example, he wrote:

> "'People of *tasawwuf* say that they see ***al-Lawh al-mahfuz***, which is called ***an-nafs al-falakiyya*** by philosophers like Ibn Sina (Avicenna). They say that the human soul, reaching perfection, unites with *an-nafs al-falakiyya* or ***al-aql al-faal*** while awake or asleep and, after uniting with one of them, which causes everything to happen in the world, the human soul becomes informed of the things existing in them. These were said not by Greek philosophers but by Ibn Sina and the like who came later. Also, *Imam* Abu Hamid al-Ghazali, Muhyiddin ibn al-Arabi and Andalusian philosopher Qutb ad-Din Muhammad ibn Sabin made statements of this sort. They are the statements of philosophers. Such things do not exist in Islam. With these arguments they diverged from the right way. They became *mulhid*s like those *mulhid*s called the Shia, *Ismailiyya*, *Qaramitis* and *Batini*s. They left the right way followed by the scholars of *Ahl as-Sunna*, by scholars of the *Hadith* and by Sunni people of *tasawwuf* like Fudayl ibn Iyad. While getting absorbed in philosophy on the one hand, they struggled, on the other, against such groups as the *Mutazila* and *Kuramiyya.* There are three groups of people of *tasawwuf*: the first group are adherent to the *Hadith* and the *Sunna*; the second group are the heretics like the

Kuramiyya; the third group are the followers of the books of **Ikhwan as-safa** and the words of Abul Hayyan. Ibn al-Arabi and Ibn Sabin and the like adopted philosophers' statements and presented them as statements of men of *tasawwuf*. Ibn Sina's book ***Akhir al-isharat ala maqamil-arifin*** contains many such statements. Also, *Al-Imam* al-Ghazali made similar statements in some of his books, such as ***Al-kitab al-madnun*** and ***Mishkat al-anwar***. In fact, his friend Abu Bakr ibn al-Arabi tried to save him from it by warning him that he had been indulging in philosophy, but his warning failed. On the other hand, *Al-Imam* al-Ghazali said that philosophers were disbelievers. Towards the end of his life he read [the *Sahih* of] *Al-Bukhari*. Some said that this made him give up the ideas he had written. Some others said that those statements were ascribed to *Al-Imam* al-Ghazali to defame him. There are various reports about *Al-Imam* al-Ghazali in this respect. Muhammad Mazari, a Maliki scholar educated in Sicily, Turtushi, an Andalusian scholar, Ibn al-Jawzi, Ibn Uqail and others said many things.'

"The assertions quoted above from Ibn Taymiyya show his ill thoughts about the scholars of *Ahl as-Sunna* clearly. Similarly, he spoke ill of even the greatest ones of the *Sahaba*t al-kiram. He misrepresented most of the scholars of *Ahl as-Sunna* as heretics. Meanwhile, as he heavily defamed the great *wali* and *qutb al-arifin Hadrat* Abul-Hasan ash-Shadhili on account of his books ***Hizb al-kabir*** and ***Hizb al-bakhr*** and degraded with foul words the superiors of *tasawwuf* such as Muhyiddin Ibn al-Arabi, Umar ibn al-Farid, Ibn Sabin and Hallaj Husain ibn Mansur, the scholars in his time declared unanimously that he was a sinner and a heretic. There were also those who issued *fatwa*s stating that he was a disbeliever.[1] A letter written to Ibn Taymiyya in 1305/705 reads:

" 'Oh my Muslim brother, who considers himself a

---

[1] The profound Islamic scholar Abd al-Ghani an-Nablusi recorded the names of these superiors of *tasawwuf* on the 363rd and 373rd pages of his book ***Al-Hadiqat an-nadiyya*** and added that each of them was a *wali* and that people who spoke ill of them were ignorant and unaware.

great scholar and the *imam* of this time! I admired you for Allah's sake. I disliked the scholars who were against you, but I was puzzled upon hearing your words that were unsuitable for admiring. Does a wise person doubt that the night begins when the sun sets? You said that you were on the right path and that you were doing ***al-amru bil-maruf wan-nahyi anil-munkar***. *Allahu Taala* knows what your purpose and intention are, but one's *ikhlas* is understood from one's deeds. Your deeds have removed the cover of your words. Deceived by people who followed their *nafs* and whose words were unreliable, you have not only defamed people living in your time but also classified the dead ones as disbelievers. Dissatisfied with attacking the successors of *Salaf as-salihin*, you have slandered the *Sahabat al-Kiram*, especially the greatest ones. Can you imagine in what a situation you will be when those great people demand their rights on the Day of Judgment? At the pulpit (*al-minbar*) in the mosque of *Jami al-jabal* in the city of Salihiyya, you said that *Hadrat* Umar (*radiy-Allahu Taala anh*) had had some wrong statements and disasters. What were the disasters? Which disasters did you hear from *Salaf as-salihin*? You say that *Hadrat* Ali (*radiy-Allahu Taala anh*) had more than 300 faults. If it had been true for *Hadrat* Ali, would you ever have had a single correct statement? Now I am beginning to act against you. I will try to protect Muslims against your wickedness, for you have exceeded the proper limit. Your torture has reached all the living and the dead. Believers must avoid your evil.'

"Taj ad-Din as-Subki listed the matters on which Ibn Taymiyya disagreed with *Salaf as-salihin*, as follows:

"1 - He said: 'Divorce in Islam (*talaq*) is not realized [so invalid]; it is necessary to pay penalty of atonement (*kaffara*, here for cancelling the divorce, paid as much as that) for an oath.' No Islamic scholar before him had said that *kaffara* would be paid.

"2 - He said: '*Talaq* uttered to a woman during her period (*haid*) is not valid.'

"3 - He said: '*Qada* (performance of a rite after its time) of a *salat* omitted knowingly is not necessary.'

"4 - He said: 'It is permissible (*mubah*) for a woman during her period to perform *tawaf* (pigrim's rite of circumambulation around the Kaba in Mecca). She need not pay *kaffara*.'

"5 - He said: '*Talaq* expressed as three *talaqs* is still one *talaq*.' For many years before saying so, however, he had said repeatedly the opposing unanimity of Muslims (*ijma al-Muslimin*).

"6 - He said: 'Taxes incompatible with Islam are *halal* for those who demand them.'

"7 - 'Such taxes collected from tradesmen takes the place of *zakat* even if not intended [for *zakat*],' he said.

"8 - He said: 'Water does not become religiously dirty (*najs*) when a mouse or the like dies in it.'

"9 - He said: 'It is permissible for a person who is *junub* (state of a Muslim needing *ghusl*, ritual ablution of whole body) to perform non-obligatory (*nafila*) ritual prayers without taking *ghusl* at night.'

"10 - He said: 'Conditions stated by the *waqif* (devotee of property to a foundation) are not taken into consideration.'

"11 - He said: 'A person who disagrees with the unanimity of Muslims (*ijma* al-*umma*) does not become a disbeliever or a sinner.'

"12 - He said: '*Allahu Taala* is *mahall-i hawadith* and is made up of particles.'

"13 - He said: 'The *Quran al-Karim* was created in the *Dhat* (Essence, Person) of *Allahu Taala*.'

"14 - He said: 'The *alam*, that is all creatures, are eternal in the past with their kinds.'

"15 - He said: '*Allahu Taala* has to create good things.'

"16 - He said: '*Allahu Taala* has a body and directions; He changes His place.'

"17 - He said: 'Hell is not eternal; it will go out at last.'

“18 - He disbelieved the fact that the prophets were sinless.

“19- He said: ‘*Rasulullah* [*sall-Allahu Taala alayhi wa sallam*] was no different from other people. It is not permissible to pray through his intercession (*shafaa*).’

“20 - He said: ‘It is sinful to go to Medina with the intention of visiting *Rasulullah*.’

“21 - He also said: ‘It is *haram* to go there to ask for intercession.’

“22 - He said: ‘The ***Tawrat*** (the original of the ***Torah***) and ***al-Injil*** (the original of the ***New Testament***) were altered not in vocabulary but in meaning.’

“Some scholars said that most of the above-quoted statements did not belong to Ibn Taymiyya, but there has been none who denied his saying that *Allahu Taala* had directions and that He was made of particles. Nevertheless, as generally agreed, his knowledge, grandeur and religiousness were considerable. A person who has *fiqh*, knowledge, justice and reason must first examine a matter and then decide about it with prudence. Especially, judging a Muslim to be a disbeliever, an apostate or a heretic or sentencing him to death requires very minute investigation and caution.”

Recently it has become fashionable to imitate Ibn Taymiyya. Some defend his heretical writings and reproduce his books, particularly ***Al-Wasita***. From beginning to end, this book is full with his ideas disagreeing with the *Quran al-Karim*, the *Hadith ash-Sharif* and the *ijma al-Muslimin*. It rouses great *fitna* and faction among readers and causes hostility among brothers. *Wahhabis* in India and ignorant people of religious position who were caught in their traps in other Muslim countries have made Ibn Taymiyya a standard-bearer for themselves and have given him such names as ‘Great *Mujtahid*’ and ‘*Shaikh al-Islam*.’ They embrace his heretical thoughts and corrupt writings in the name of the Religion and belief. For stopping this horrifying current, which brings about faction among Muslims and demolishes Islam from within, we must read the valuable books written by the scholars of *Ahl as-Sunna* which refute and rebut him with documents. Among this valuable literature, the book ***Shifa as-siqam fi ziyarati khayri l-***

anam by the great *imam* and the profoundly learned scholar Taqi ad-Din as-Subki (rahmat-Allahi Taala alayh) invalidated Ibn Taymiyya's heretical ideas, destroyed his faction and exposed his obstinacy. It prevents the spreading of his evil intentions and wrong beliefs.

GLOSSARY

Numbers below refer to the pages on which the entries are defined in the text. Words related to *tasawwuf* can be learned best from *Hadrat al-Imam ar-Rabbani*'s *Al-Maktubat.*

-adillat ash-Shariyya: four sources of Islamic knowledge, namely the *Quran al-Karim*, the *Hadith ash-Sharif, ijma al-Umma* and *qiyas al-fuqaha.*

ahl al-bida: heretics, people of heresy, 16, 32, 114.

Ahl as-Sunna(t wal-Jamaa): 'People of the Prophet and his Companions'; *Sunni* Muslims (Sunnis) with original, correct belief, so the ***Firqat an-najiyya,*** the largest group of Muslims who will be 'protected' from Hell, 9; the scholars (*ulama*) of: 6.

aimmat al-madhahib: founding *imams* of the four *madhhabs.*

alam: 97.

alayhimus-salam: (prayer for the prophets) 'May peace be upon them'.

alim, âlim: (pl. **ulama**) scholar, one trained in Islamic sciences; **Alîm:** the Omniscient.

Allahu Taala: Allah, the Supreme and non-deficient.

amal: deeds, acts, rituals, worship; *fiqh*, *ibadat*; 30, 92 106.

Amin: Amen.

-amru bil-maruf wan-nahyi anil-munkar: duty of teaching *Allahu Taala*'s commands and preventing His prohibitions.

arif: a scholar who knows what is possible to know of *marifa*, the knowledge about *Allahu Taala*'s *Dhat* and Attributes.

-***Arsh***, 46.

Ashari, Ashariyya: 73, 104.

Astaghfirullah: see *istighfar;* 6, 15.

awliya: pl. of **wali**, one loved and protected by *Allahu Taala.*

awrat: private body parts, 27, 29.

ayat (***karima***)*:* a statement or a sentence of the *Quran al-Karim.*

Azrail: 38.

-Basmala: the Arabc phrase, "In the name of Allah, the Compassionate, the Merciful."

bida: heresy.

bint: daughter of.

bitha (year of) a prophet's appointment for calling people to the right path; the ***Bitha***, that of Muhammad (*alayhis-salam).*

-Dhat: 'Essence, Self, Person, Personality' of *Allahu Taala.*

faqih: 35.

fard: *Allahu Taala*'s ordinances, so obligatory teachings or rituals that have to be performed; a kind of rules within the *salat* or other rituals: 8, 13, 15.

fatwa: ruling made on a religious matter by Islamic scholars, 47.

fiqh: (methodologic science of) knowledge dealing with what Muslims should do and should not do; *ibadat.*

-Firqat ad-dalla: 'the heretical group', the ***Shii***s (Shiites, Shia); 9.

-Firqat an-najiyya: 9.

fitna: widespreading of statements or actions harming Muslims and Islam; mischief.

furu (ad-Din): Islamic rules of practices compared to beliefs, 13,59.

hadith (sharif): (pl. ***ahadith sharif***) an honorable saying of Muhammad *alayhis-salam*; ***al-Hadith (ash-Sharif),*** all 'the Honorable *ahadith*' as a whole; science of the *Hadith*; ***hadith qudsi:*** a *hadith sharif* with meaning by *Allahu Taala* but with words by Muhammad (*alayhis-salam*).

hâdith: that which has been created later; 20, 21, 39, 97.

Hadrat: expression of honor and respect used for *Alahu Taala*, the prophets and scholars.

hajj: 26.

halal: (act, thing) permitted in Islam; non-*haram*.

haram: *(act, thing)* forbidden, to be avoided, in Islam; a prohibition, 8, 13, 15.

-Hijra: the Hegira, 24; ***Hijri*** (of the Hegira) ***Kamari***, Muslim Lunar (AH) calendar.

ibada: *(pl.* ***ibadat****)* worship, rituals; thanking *Allahu Taala*, that is, following Muhammad (*alayhis-salam*), 30, 72 92.

ibn: the son of.

ijma (al-Muslimin, al-Umma): consensus, unanimity of Muslims, esp. of *Salaf as-salihin*. See *adilla.*

ijtihad: 53.

ikhlas: sincere piousness; quality, intention or state of, doing everything only for *Allahu Taala*'s sake.

ilm: (branch of) knowledge, 92; ***ilm al-hal***, (books of) Islamic teachings (of one *madhhab*) ordered to be learned by every Muslim; ***ilm al-kalam***: knowledge of *iman*, beliefs.

imam: a) profound scholar ***(alim)****;* founder of a *madhhab (imam al-madhhab, mujtahid imam);* ***al-Imam al-Azam***: 'Most Superior Leader', title for Abu Hanifa, 71; ***al-Imam ar-Rabbani:*** 'scholar owning Divine Knowledge', title for Ahmad al-Faruqi as-Sirindi; b) leader in congregational *salat*; c) caliph.

iman: belief; see ***itiqad.***

insha-Allahu Taala: 'if *Allahu Taala* wills'. 4, 30.

islam: 13, 23; **Islam**, 13.

istighfar: Begging *Allahu Taala* for forgiveness of unbelief and sins by saying '*Astaghfirullah*'.

itiqad: (system of) beliefs or tenets; creed, faith; *iman, aqaid, furu.*

jamaa: union, community; *as-Sahabat al-Kiram* as in *Ahl as-Sunnat wal-Jamaa*; congregation, Muslims except the *imam* in a mosque.

***jihad*:** fight against non-Muslims or against the *nafs* to convert to Islam, 70.

***kafir*:** unbeliever, who does not believe in even one of the Islamic teachings, 15.

kalam: speech, word; the knowledge of *iman.*

kalimat ash-shahada: 24.

kalimat at-tawhid*:** the sentence 'La ilaha illa'llah Muhammadun Rasulullah,***' (*Allahu Taala* exists and is One. Muhammad *alayhis-salam* is the Prophet sent by *Allahu Taala*); 13.

kasb: 82-83.

kashf: inspired unveiling of Divine mysteries; discovery.

Khalaf (as-sadiqin): 'Successors, the Faithful'; those scholars of *Ahl as-Sunna* succeeding *Salaf as-salihin*; 105.

***Khidir*:** 45.

***khutba*:** homily delivered at the pulpit by the *imam* at Friday and Islamic festival prayers and recited in Arabic all over the world (sinful if read in another language).

***kiraman katibin*:** incorruptible record-keeping angels, 38.

***La ilaha illa'llah*:** 8, 9, 13.

la-madhhabi: (those) following none of the four *madhhab*s of *Ahl as-Sunna*; non-Sunnis; ***la-madhhabism***, 9, 60.

-***Lawh al-mahfuz:*** place where Divine Knowledge is recorded in eternal past.

maal: 8, 67.

***madhhab*:** system of the teachings in each Islamic schools of the four profound scholars of Islam; (in belief) 73; (in practice) 71, 72.

-***Madinat al-Munawwara:*** the Illuminated City of Medina.

-***Mahdi*:** 74.

-***Makkat al-Mukarram:*** the Honorable City of Mecca, the birthplace of Muhammad *alayhis-salam.*

makruh: (act, thing) improper, disliked and abstained by the Prophet.

mandub: (act, thing) that brings *thawab* if done, but neither sin if omitted nor unbelief if disliked; also called ***adab*** or ***mustahab***.

maqbul: 92.

Maturidiyya: 73, 104.

Mawlid: birth, birthday, birthday celebration of, or long poems of elogizing, Prophet Muhammad (*alayhis-salam*).

-Miraj: 46.

mubah: (thing, act) permitted, permissible; 92.

mufti: great scholar authorized to issue *fatwa*.

mujiza: miracle, 40.

mujtahid: 53; see *imam*.

mulhid: 34.

mumkin: 20; ***mumkin al-wujud***: 99.

munafiq: hypocrite, one hiding one's disbelief.

muqallid: (follower of) one adhering to a *madhhab*, 59.

murshid: a scholar and a *wali* guiding Muslims to correct path and training them for perfection.

-Mutazila: one of the 72 groups that deviated from *Ahl as-Sunna*, 83.

nafs: a malignant force in humans that is hostile to *Allahu Taala*; human desires, 87.

nass: general term for an *ayat karima* or a *hadith sharif*; the ***Nass,*** reference to the *Quran al-Karim* and the *Hadith ash-Sharif* as a whole.

nisab: 26.

qada: a) 78; b) 117.

qadar: 78, 90.

qaddas-Allahu Taala asrarahum ajmain: "May *Allahu Taala* make all their mystiques decent, sacred and blessed!"

qiyas (al-fuqaha): (conclusion drawn by a *mujtahid* through) likening or comparing an affair not clearly stated in the *Nass*.

quddisa sirruh: "May *Allahu Taala* make his mystiques decent, sacred and blessed!"

-***Quran al-Karim:*** *The Gracious Koran*, 14.

radiy-Allahu Taala anh: (prayer said for the Sahaba) "May *Allahu Taala* be pleased with him."

rahimahu'llahu Taala, ***rahmatullahi alayh***: "May *Allahu Taala* bless him."

rasul: (pl. ***rusul***) a messenger or a prophet appointed by *Allahu Taala*, 42, 43; ***Rasul-Allah, Rasulullah***: the Prophet Muhammad (*alayhis-salam*).

rusul: pl. of ***rasul***.

-***Sahaba(t al-Kiram)*** (or ***As'hab al-Kiram***): the Grand Companions of the Prophet.

sahih: a) valid, suitable, 92; b) genuine, authentic.

Salaf (as-salihin): 'Predecessors the Pious', Muslims of the first two centuries; a designation for the *Sahabat al-Kiram* and the *Tabiun*; 104.

salat: ritual prayers in Islam, 25.

salawat: invocation; expressing praise and blessings upon Prophet Muhammad (*alayhis-salam*), 3.

salih (pl. ***sulaha***): (one) pious, avoiding sins.

sall-Allahu alayhi wa sallam: (prayer said for the Prophet) "May *Allahu Taala* grant peace and honor on he and his family."

shuhud: seeing the examples/*mithal*s through the 'eyes' of their hearts.

-***Sifat adh-Dhatiyya:*** (Personal Attributes) of *Allahu Taala*, p. 17, 19.

-***Sifat ath-Thubutiyya***: those Divine Attributes partially exemplified in creatures, see p. 19, 21, 22, 35.

sulaha: (pl. of *salih)* the pious avoiding sinning.

sunna: (act, thing) that, though not commanded by *Allahu Taala*, done and liked by the Prophet as an *ibada* (there is *thawab* if done, but no sin if omitted, yet it causes sin if continually omitted and disbelief if disliked); such kind of rules within the *salat* or other rituals; the ***Sunna:*** a) (with *fard*) all the *sunna*s as a whole; b) (with the Book or the *Quran al-Karim*) the *Hadith ash-Sharif;* c) *fiqh*, Islam.

sura(t): a chapter of the *Quran al-Karim.*

Taba at-Tabiin: 106, 112.

-*Tabiun (al-Izam)*: the Promoted [immediate] Followers of the *Sahabat al-Kiram*, 106.

Tabligh Jamaa: 48.

tafsir: (the science of) explanations of the *Quran al-Karim.*

taqwa: protecting oneself from committing *haram.*

tasawwuf: branch of knowledge and (after adapting oneself to *fiqh*) practice of the manners of the Prophet (*alayhis-salam*) which strengthens *iman*, makes the practice of *fiqh* easy and provides one to attain *marifa.*

tawatur: successive, repetitive, multi-sourced, so doubtlessly authentic, widespread reporting of original Islamic information; reports that were told in the same words by all the trustworthy people of each century for whom it was impossible to agree on falsehood and that produced absolute knowledge; such consensus or unanimity.

tawba: 6.

tawil: interpreting suitably with Islam, 33, 39.

thawab: unit of, reward promised to be given in the next world by *Allahu Taala* as a recompense for the doing and saying of what He likes.

ulama: (pl. of *alim*) scholars, especially of Islamic knowledge.

umma: community of followers of a prophet; the *Umma*, that of Muhammad (alayhis-salam), 43.

Wahhabi(sm): 9, 56.

wahy: Divine revelation to the prophets.

wajib: (act, thing) never omitted by the Prophet, so almost as compulsory as *fard* and not to be omitted; a kind of rules within the *salat* or other rituals. ***Wajib* (*al-wujud*):** 20, 100.

wali: *(pl.* ***awliya****)* one loved and protected by *Allahu Taala.*

zindiq: one who not only hides one's disbelief but also pretends to be a Muslim and thereby tries to deceive Muslims, 34, 58.